CREATIVE
BEAD JEWELRY

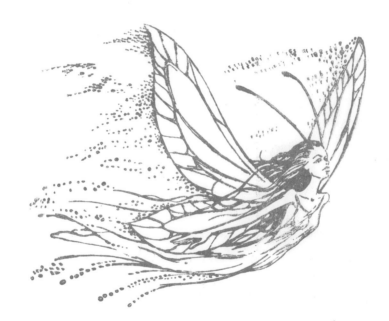

This book belongs to
Lilyen L. Chesser

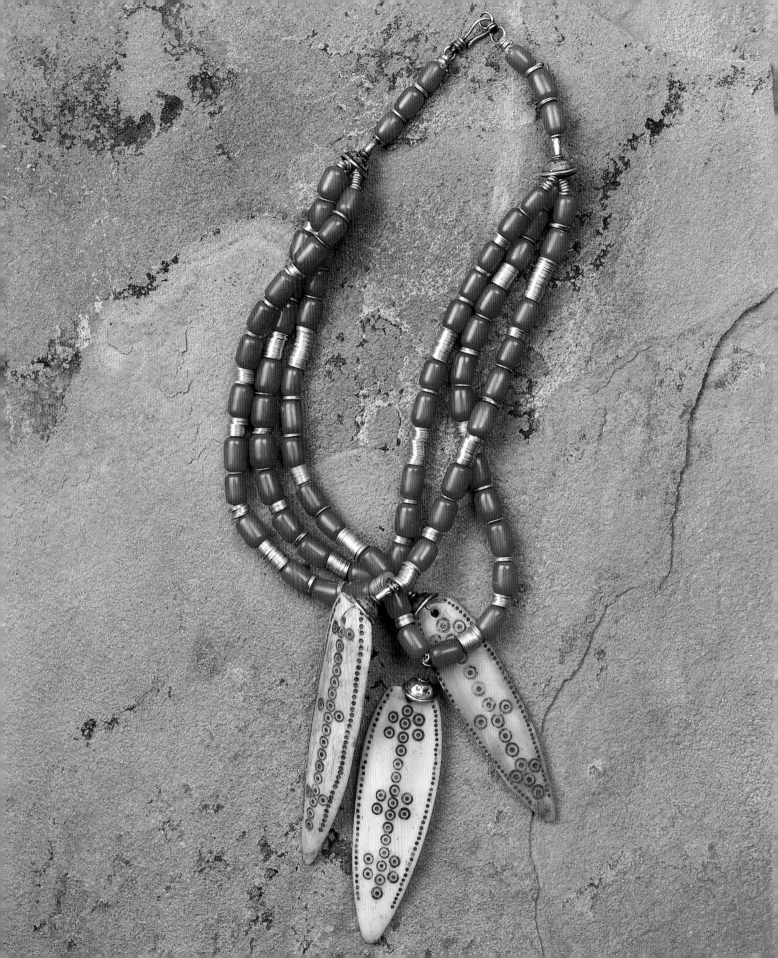

CREATIVE
BEAD JEWELRY

Weaving ◆ *Looming* ◆ *Stringing* ◆ *Wiring*
Making Beads

CAROL TAYLOR

Sterling Publishing Co., Inc.   New York
A STERLING/LARK BOOK

Art Direction, Illustrations, and Production: Chris Colando
Photographer: Evan Bracken

Library of Congress Cataloging-in-Publication Data
Taylor, Carol
     Creative bead jewelry: stringing, wiring, weaving, looming,
  making beads / by Carol Taylor
        p.   cm.
     "A Sterling/Lark book."
     Includes index.
     ISBN 0-8069-1306-1
     1. Beadwork. 2. Jewelry making. I. Title.
TT860.T39 1995   95-4595
745.594'2- -dc20   CIP

10 9 8 7 6 5 4 3 2 1

A Sterling/Lark Book

Published by Sterling Publishing Co., Inc.
387 Park Ave. South, New York, NY 10016

Created and produced by Altamont Press, Inc.
50 College St., Asheville, NC 28801

Distributed in Canada by Sterling Publishing, c/o Canadian Manda Group,
One Atlantic Ave., Suite 105, Toronto, Ontario, Canada M6K 3E7

Distributed in Great Britain and Europe by Cassell PLC, Wellington House,
125 Strand, London, England WC2R OBB

Distributed in Australia by Capricorn Link (Australia) Pty Ltd., P.O.Box 6651, Baulkham Hills
Business Centre, NSW, Australia 2153

Printed in Hong Kong

ISBN 0-8069-1306-1

CONTENTS

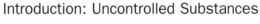

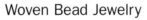

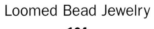

UNCONTROLLED SUBSTANCES

APPROACH ANY VETERAN BEADER—ANY LOVER, COLLECTOR, STRINGER, WEAVER, LOOMER, OR MAKER OF BEADS—AND IF YOU'RE A NEWCOMER TO THE CRAFT, YOU WILL INVARIABLY HEAR, "WATCH OUT! BEADS ARE ADDICTIVE!"

In the interests of full disclosure, we'd like to issue the same warning right up front. Run your hand through one little tray of brilliant beads...wander into one seedy bead store, with its seductive strands from Europe, Africa, Asia, and the Americas...admire just a few gorgeous creations of glass, silver, porcelain, bone, brass, horn, wood, semi-precious stones...

You're doomed.

How can you tell if you're hooked? Ask yourself these questions—and don't flinch from the answers.

WOODEN BEADS

DO YOU TELL YOURSELF THAT YOU CAN STOP BEADING ANY TIME YOU WANT TO... BUT YOU KEEP RIGHT ON?

Oh sure, maybe you quit for a day or two. Then the Saturday flea market rolls around, and you head out "just to look." There lies an old bracelet with one gorgeous bead on it. You buy the bracelet for a song and design a handsome, contemporary necklace around that one great bead.

Ah, well. Maybe you'll quit on Monday.

DO YOU GET UP IN THE MIDDLE OF THE NIGHT TO BEAD?

You're peacefully drifting off when you remember the tube of tiny seed beads you bought this afternoon...the ones with the indefinable color somewhere between pink and peach and rose...the ones that shimmer in the softest light. Before reason can assert itself, you're out of bed and seated at the kitchen table, laying out your design.

Another midnight beader.

HAS YOUR BEADING CAUSED TROUBLE AT WORK?

You wear one too many gorgeous necklaces on the job...and your colleagues' affection turns to envy. You dress up one too many outfits with a perfectly matched pair of woven earrings...and your boss

HAND-WORKED
SILVER BEADS

(unaware that each pair cost less than a cup of coffee) decides you're overpaid.

Your next raise is history.

ARE BEADS AFFECTING YOUR FINANCIAL SECURITY?

You are the hardest of the hard core. Beads are wonderfully collectible, not just because they're beautiful, but because they're inexpensive (compared to teapots, say, or Van Goghs). If you're spending yourself into the poorhouse, your collection must approximate the pyramids.

Seek professional help immediately.

DO YOU FEEL AS IF YOU ARE THE ONLY PERSON IN THE WORLD WHOSE BEADING IS OUT OF CONTROL?

It's not true. Millions of us love these miniature splashes of color. We sort them, treasure them, assemble and disassemble our favorites into various pieces of jewelry. We travel to new cities and flip eagerly through the phone book, looking for bead stores. We send for mail-order catalogs and order a handful here, a handful there.

You are not alone.

If you answered no to these five questions, try to be compassionate toward those of us who answered yes to all of them. You may not think you know any beaders, but you do. We are your older sisters, your favorite aunts, your long-lost cousins. We are your employers, your accountants, your lawyers, your check-out clerks.

We are everywhere.

GLASS BEADS

BEADING BASICS

To make stunning bead jewelry, you'll need a few beads and a few ways to hold them together.

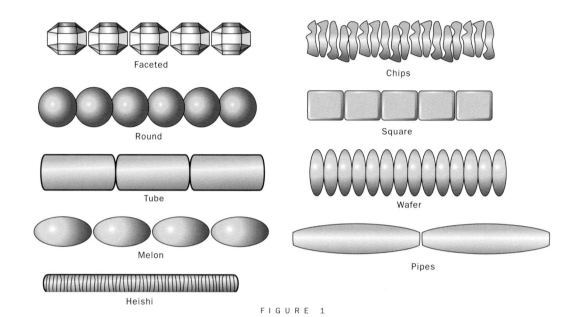

FIGURE 1

BEADS

Bone, horn, wood, metal, precious and semi-precious stones, rock, shell, clay, glass, paper, fabric—if it can be carved, molded, or drilled, people have made beads out of it. Today, beads are available in a range of colors, materials, and shapes (see Figure 1) to suit every conceivable taste.

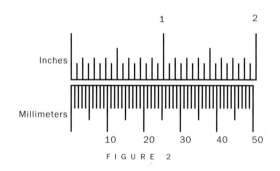

FIGURE 2

Bead Sizes

Beads are measured in millimeters. If you're accustomed to inches, note the comparison in Figure 2. Note also the circles in Figure 3, which are shown actual size.

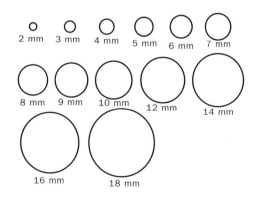

FIGURE 3

Seed Beads

Named for the seeds they resemble, these small (sometimes tiny) glass beads are sized according to number; the higher the number, the smaller the bead. Most widely available are size 6 (often written 6˚) and size 11. Size 11s are most popular for weaving and looming.

Seed beads are available in a variety of finishes from matte to metallic, a riot of colors, and a number of shapes. Bugle beads are long, narrow tubes. Cut beads are faceted; they add a marvelous shimmer. Delicas are cylindrical, almost square in shape, about the size of a size 12 seed bead. Their large holes, regular shape, and gorgeous colors make them delightful to work with.

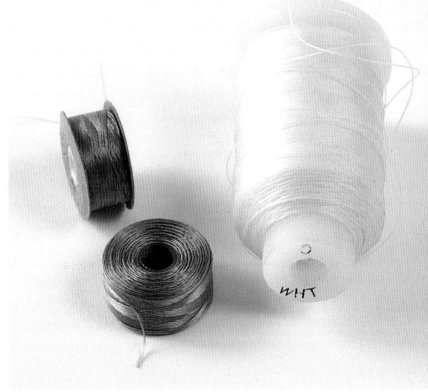

BEAD THREAD

CORD

Beads hang happily from various materials.

Bead Thread

Good bead thread is thin enough to go through the holes in the beads (several times if necessary) and strong enough to hold them together. For a strung necklace, it should be supple enough to drape gracefully. If the jewelry needs to last longer than tonight's outfit, the thread should resist fraying, abrasion, and (if you're using sharp or metal beads) cutting. It's helpful if it is durable and stretch resistant. Match the thread color to the beads. If no match is possible, select a color lighter than the beads, rather than darker.

CLOCKWISE FROM TOP: SIZE 11 SEED BEADS, DELICA BEADS, SIZE 6 MATTE SEEDS, SIZE 3.3 CYLINDERS

The best bead threads are the new synthetics. Multifilament nylon thread is the choice of most weavers of seed beads. Strong, synthetic bead cord is beloved by stringers. Read a couple of catalogs and ask for specific brand name advice at your local store.

Most bead thread requires a needle on the end of it.

Monofilament

Better for catching fish than stringing beads, monofilament is not strongly recommended. It breaks, stretches, and is easily cut. (A lot of marvelous Third World jewelry is strung on monofilament; be prepared to restring it.) On the other hand, it requires no needle and it's virtually trans-

FLAT LEATHER
THONG & WAXED
LINEN CORD

DESIGN:
LONNIE LOVNESS

WAXED LINEN CORD

DESIGN: LONNIE LOVNESS

parent and thus invisible in translucent beads. It's useful for trying out designs before actually stringing the beads.

Tigertail

This tiny steel cable coated with nylon is tough, flexible, and strong—excellent for stringing beads. Because it's stiff, it requires no needle, and, while it doesn't knot well, it's easy to finish with crimp beads. On the other hand, it has a mind of its own—a stiffness—so it kinks easily and it doesn't drape well with small, lightweight beads.

Decorative Cords

While bead thread and tigertail should be invisible in the finished jewelry, decorative cords can be part of the final design.

LEFT: LARGE-
EYED, FLEXIBLE
NEEDLES. RIGHT:
SLENDER, RIGID
NEEDLES.

Leather cord strings well and knots easily. It complements large or ethnic beads and casual jewelry. Flat leather thong has an appealing cowboy look.

Waxed linen cord comes in a variety of colors. It knots well and fits most standard glass beads.

Rattail (ignore the name) is an attractive, dressy, satin-like cord available in a wide range of colors.

NEEDLES

One advantage of heavy synthetic cord is that you can dip the end in instant glue to stiffen it and proceed to string beads. For most bead thread, however, you'll need a needle.

Big-eyed and flexible, twisted-wire needles are easy to thread and a pleasure to use. They hold multiple threads without a murmur. The large eye closes up when it's forced through a bead, but an awl or pin can reopen it for the next project. This needle is too big and bendable for weaving seed beads.

For weaving (and for stringing small-holed beads), you'll need beading needles that resemble ordinary sewing "sharps." They are numbered according to size—10, 13, and 15, for example. The larger the number, the thinner the needle. For ease of threading, use the largest needle that will go through your beads. Theoretically, needle numbers and seed bead numbers match. (A size 11 needle will go through a size 11 seed bead but not necessarily through a size 14.)

If you can thread a small-eyed needle, you can master any beading stitch ever devised. You can probably invent your own. To up your odds, cut the thread at an angle, moisten it, and squeeze it flat. Moisten the eye of the needle as well.

CLOCKWISE FROM LEFT: ROUND-NOSE PLIERS, CHAIN-NOSE PLIERS, WIRE CUTTERS

Glue

Glues are indispensable. The most common, known as bead glue or bead cement, comes in a small tube. Its uses are many, but its most important function is to seal knots in thread, which will merrily unravel if left unglued. Any knot you make should get a dab of cement. Although bead cement comes with a pointed applicator, it's not pointed enough. Use a needle or straight pin to add a tiny dab to every knot you make, being careful not to get glue on the beads. (Clear nail polish also works well on knots.)

An incredibly useful glue is an industrial-strength adhesive and sealant. It comes in large tubes and is available in most bead stores. It will glue almost anything to almost anything else.

If you work with leather, you'll need either leather glue or a white craft glue that remains flexible after it dries.

CUTTERS AND PLIERS

To work with wire and metal findings, you'll need a few basic tools.

Wire cutters should cut flush, allowing you to nip off "burrs"—tiny wire ends that can snag clothing and skin.

Round-nose pliers are essential for making loops.

Chain-nose pliers are rounded on the outside surfaces but flat on the inside, gripping surface, enabling you to grip the wire.

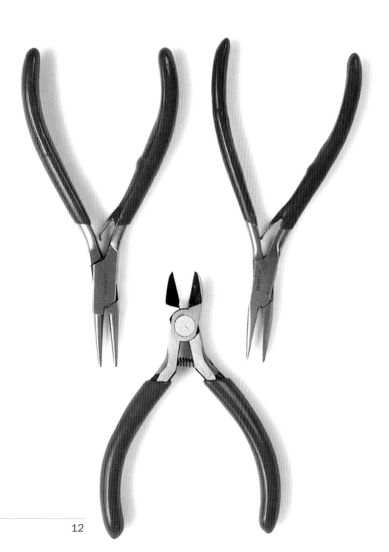

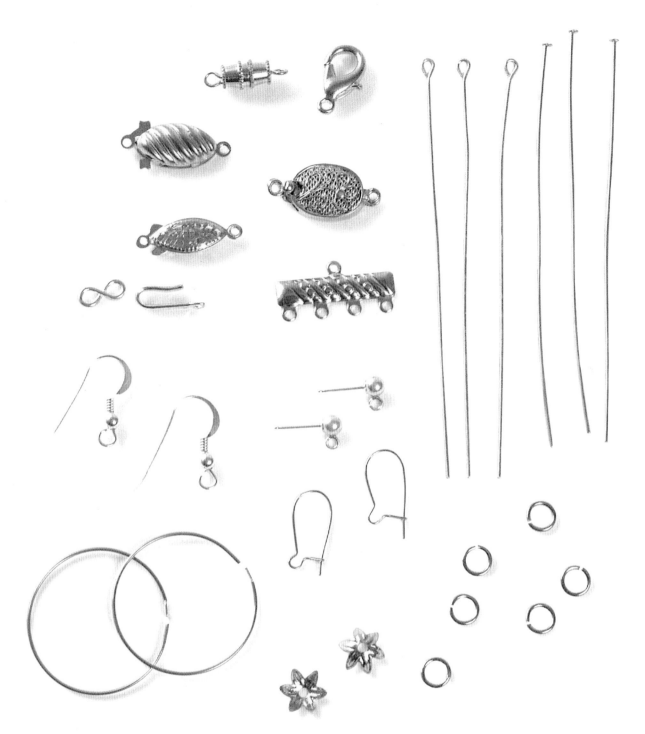

GENERAL FINDINGS

Findings are the manufactured components that turn beads into jewelry. They are sold in bead shops and craft stores worldwide.

Bead Caps

A bead cap cups the end of a bead, hiding the hole and providing a finished look.

Head Pins and Eye Pins

These are normally sold by the dozen, and that's the way you'll use them. Available in various sizes, they are straight pieces of wire with a "stopper" on one end to keep the beads from falling off. A head pin has a flat head (much like a nail head); an eye pin has a loop, or eye. Loop the other end of the pin around whatever you want to attach it to.

CLOCKWISE FROM
TOP LEFT:

ASSORTED CLASPS,
EYE PINS,
HEAD PINS,
JUMP RINGS AND
SPLIT RINGS,
BEAD CAPS,
VARIOUS EARRING
FINDINGS

Jump Rings

Jump rings are simply wire circles. (Many people make their own.) One variant, known as a split ring, resembles a tiny key ring. Jump rings are useful for connecting things—for example, a bead tip to a clasp or a charm to a bracelet.

A jump ring is slit somewhere on its circumference, and you'll need to pry it open to use it. If you open it by enlarging the circle—that is, spreading its ends farther apart—you'll weaken the ring. Instead, using two pairs of pliers, twist the ring open, forcing one end forward and one end back. See Figure 4. Close the ring by reversing that movement.

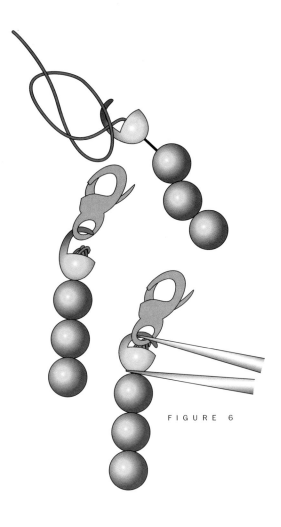

FIGURE 6

To finish a string of beads with a jump ring, take the needle and thread through the ring, wrapping the thread twice. Then needle back through several beads and knot the thread. See Figure 5. Needle back through several more beads and knot again. Clip the tails and dot the knots with bead cement. Open the jump ring, attach it to a clasp, then reclose it.

NECKLACE AND BRACELET FINDINGS

At each end of a string of beads will be... well ... string. Now what?

FIGURE 4

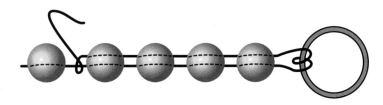

FIGURE 5

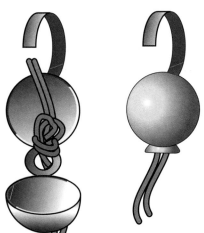

FIGURE 7

CLASPS

Available in dozens of styles, clasps allow you to open and close a necklace or bracelet. Every clasp has a loop; if the clasp has two parts, each part will have a loop. Various pieces of hardware will bridge string to clasp.

Bead Tips

Most useful for single-strand necklaces, bead tips finish jewelry that is strung on bead thread. They hold and hide the knots and supply metal loops for attaching to the clasp.

To use them, take the needle and thread through a bead tip, with the hook facing outward, toward the end of the necklace. Tie the thread in a knot around a needle or pin, using it to coax the knot into the cup of the bead tip. Knot again. Dot the knots with bead cement or clear nail polish and clip the thread tail close to the knot. Take the bead tip's hook through the clasp and close the hook with chain-nose pliers. See Figure 6.

A clamshell bead tip hides the knot more effectively. Follow the directions above, but after the thread is knotted and glued, close the clamshell with chain-nose pliers. See Figure 7.

You can add the first bead tip, then the beads, then the second bead tip. If you're making a symmetrical necklace—especially if you're making up the design as you go along—it is sometimes easier to string all the beads, then attach both bead tips.

Crimp Beads

When compressed (or "crimped"), crimp beads hold tightly onto what's inside. They're used primarily on tigertail, which knots poorly.

String a crimp bead onto the end of the tigertail, then string on a clasp. Bring the tigertail back

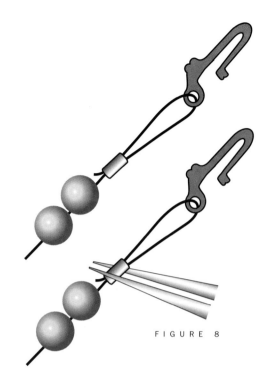

FIGURE 8

through the crimp bead, forming a loop around the clasp. Slide the crimp bead tight up against the clasp and flatten the crimp bead with chain-nose pliers. See Figure 8. Trim the tigertail and thread the cut end back through a few beads.

EARRING FINDINGS

There are endless ways to attach beads to ears: posts, French wires, kidney wires, and for the unpierced among us, clips and screws.

For your first few projects, select an ear finding with a loop that can be opened and closed. That way you can finish the beading, open the loop on the finding, add the beadwork, and reclose the loop. If the loop on the finding won't open, you'll have to incorporate it into the beading. While not a major problem, it's somewhat awkward at first.

Pin Backs

Usually, a pin back consists of a flat bar with holes along its length. At each end is a protruding piece of hardware. You can simply glue the finding to the back of your beadwork (this is, after all, the back) or finish it more carefully.

If your piece has a leather backing, glue the pin back to the leather and allow it to dry. Lay a second piece of leather over the pin back and mark the locations of the two projecting ends. Cut a hole for each end. Open the pin and fit the leather down over the back, guiding the hardware through the holes. Glue the second piece of leather to the first, with the right side facing out.

Barrette Backs

A barrette back is a long metal strip with projecting hardware at each end. The barrettes in this book consist of beadwork on leather or chamois. The barrette back is glued to the back of the beadwork, then covered with another piece of leather that has holes at each end for the hardware to come through.

A FLAT PIN BACK, GLUED TO THE BACK OF A PIN, THEN COVERED WITH LEATHER TO FINISH; A SAFETY-STYLE PIN WITH LOOPS FOR A BEAD; A BARRETTE BACK

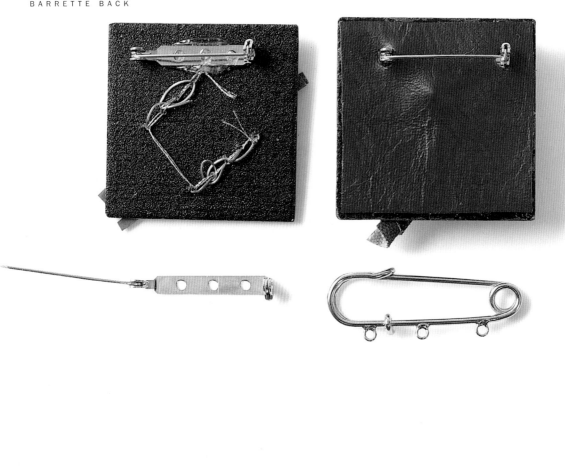

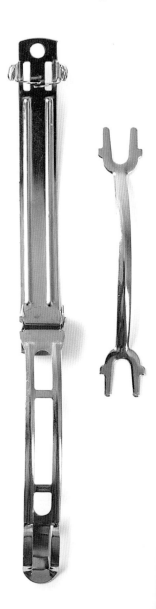

DESIGN

NUMBER.

String a few beads or a few dozen. The results will
be completely different but equally pleasing.

DESIGN: MADISON MACLAREN

DESIGN: LESLIE BRUNTSCH

17

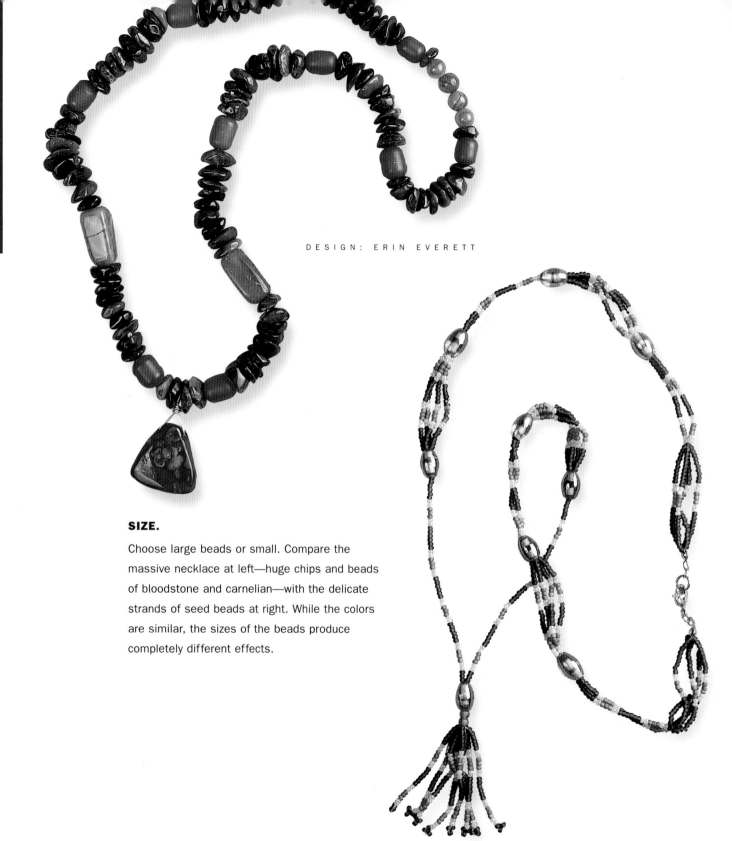

DESIGN: ERIN EVERETT

DESIGN: BARBARA WRIGHT

SIZE.

Choose large beads or small. Compare the massive necklace at left—huge chips and beads of bloodstone and carnelian—with the delicate strands of seed beads at right. While the colors are similar, the sizes of the beads produce completely different effects.

SHAPE.

Round isn't everything. This wired necklace includes only two materials—unakite and silver—but a myriad of shapes: chips, triangles, cylinders, melons, globes, and a central doughnut.

DESIGN: GALEN MADARAS

COLOR.

For these simple Comanche earrings, compare the dressy black and gold with the casual pale blue and white.

DESIGN: MARY YOUNG SMITH

STRINGING BASICS

BEADS STRUNG ON A CORD—WHAT COULD BE SIMPLER? WHILE THEY CAN BE STRUNG IN ANY ORDER THAT PLEASES THE STRINGER, FIGURE 1 ILLUSTRATES SOME COMMON DESIGNS.

BEADING BOARD

While not essential, an inexpensive beading board is extremely useful. It allows you to lay out a single- or multistrand necklace with precision, holding the beads in place and indicating where each one will fall on the finished piece. In its absence, lay the beads out on a towel.

Making a Continuous Necklace

If a necklace is at least 24 inches (61.5 cm) long—long enough to go over your head—its ends can be

A BEADING BOARD FOR SINGLE OR MULTIPLE STRANDS.

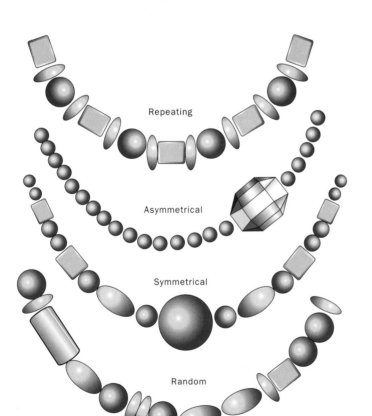

Repeating

Asymmetrical

Symmetrical

Random

joined without a clasp. Select strong, good-quality bead thread that knots easily and well.

1 Cut a piece of thread twice the length of the finished necklace plus 8 inches (20.5 cm) and string it on a beading needle. Wax the thread and double it, but don't knot it. Tape or clip the tail ends so the beads won't fall off.

2 String the beads for the necklace.

3 When the beads are strung, leave the first needle on the thread. Add another needle onto the tail threads, taking both through the eye.

4 Cross-thread the beads—that is, take each needle through a few beads on the opposite end.

FIGURE 1

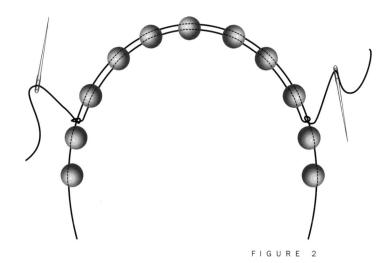

5 Tie each tail to the necklace between two beads, using a double knot. See Figure 2.

6 Take each needle through a few more beads and knot again. Repeat if desired.

7 Dot the knots with bead cement or clear nail polish. If possible, use a large needle to nudge each knot into the hole of an adjacent bead.

MULTISTRAND NECKLACES

There are various ways to make a necklace (or bracelet) of several strands.

Spacers and Multistrand Clasps

Available in a variety of materials, spacers are rigid bars with two to five holes. Thread a strand of beads through each hole, and the spacer will hold them in the right order. Clasps are available with multiple loops.

Using Cones

Cones are a distinctive and attractive way to finish

F I G U R E   2

a multistrand necklace. Just be sure that the beads at each end are small enough to fit into a cone.

1. Select a large eye pin. To make your own, cut a piece of 20- or 22-gauge wire about 1-1/2 inches (4 cm) longer than the cone and make a loop at one end of the wire, using round-nose pliers.

2. Tie the bead threads onto the wire loop, using a secure double knot. Trim the thread ends and add a dab of bead cement to the knot.

3. Thread the cone onto the wire, covering both the knot and the loop of wire. See Figure 3.

4. Make a loop in the remaining wire end, twisting

STERLING SILVER SPACERS FROM SRI-LANKA

F I G U R E   3

the wire around itself two or three times. Trim the wire end. Attach the loop to a jump ring or clasp.

VARIABLE-STRAND NECKLACES

A necklace that alternates between a single strand and multiple strands is nifty-looking and comfortable; there's only one strand of beads at the back of your neck. Large-holed beads are essential.

Cut as many pieces of thread as the maximum number of strands that the necklace will have—let's say six. Thread all six pieces of thread onto a large-eyed, twisted-wire needle, and tape or clip the ends so the beads don't fall off. Treating the six threads as one, string on the beads for the left-hand single strand.

When the single strand is as long as you want it, remove the threads from the needle. Add a needle to each piece of thread. (Since each needle will hold only one thread, smaller-eyed, rigid needles will do fine. If the beads are small, they're essen-

LONG, STRAIGHT FRINGE

DESIGN: MARY YOUNG SMITH

tial.) String beads onto each separate thread until the multiple strands are as long as you want them.

Remove the six needles from the threads. String all six threads onto the twisted-wire needle. Again treating the six threads as one, string the beads for the single strand on the right side of the necklace. Add a clasp.

MAKING FRINGE

If you've ever swept dramatically through a bead curtain, you know the value of fringe. Free-swinging strands of beads add movement and interest to beaded jewelry.

To begin the fringe, anchor a long thread to the jewelry (see individual project instructions) and add a needle.

String on beads as desired; the more beads, the longer the fringe. At the bottom, string on a larger

VARIABLE-STRAND
NECKLACE

DESIGN: SARAH
K. YOUNG

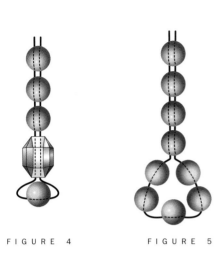

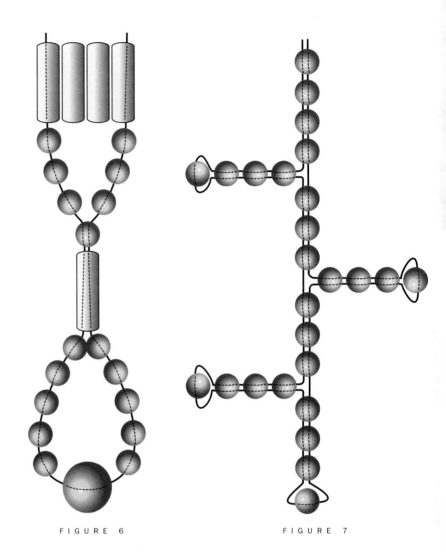

FIGURE 4   FIGURE 5

FIGURE 6   FIGURE 7

bead for weight, then another small bead. Take the thread around the small bead, then back up through all the previous beads. See Figure 4.

Instead of a large bead, end the strand with a loop of beads. The more beads, the larger the loop. See Figure 5. Or hang the fringe from two beads that are farther apart. See Figure 6.

BRANCHED FRINGE

String on enough beads for the full length of the fringe, keeping in mind that it will shorten somewhat as you work. Take the thread around the last bead and back up through several beads—let's say three.

Bring the needle out of the main stem and string on the beads for a side twig—let's say four. Go around the last bead and back up through the twig beads. Then rejoin the main stem, taking the needle back up as many beads as you like. Exit again when you're ready for another twig. See Figure 7.

The fringe will hang better if the twigs fall on different sides of the stem.

BRANCHED FRINGE

DESIGN: GINI WILLIAMS

23

LEATHER CLASPS WITH BEAD EDGING.

DESIGN: CHERI LYNN WALTZ

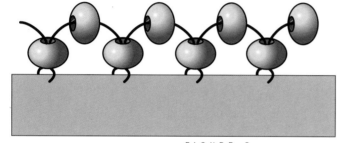

FIGURE 8

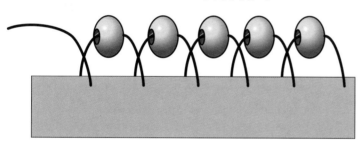

FIGURE 9

BEAD EDGINGS

When joining two pieces of leather, a simple running stitch will often serve, especially if a row of beads covers the joined edges. Another alternative is a venerable Native American technique called a bead edging.

Lay the two pieces of leather so that the edges are aligned. For a two-bead edging, take the needle through a bead, then through both pieces of leather, then up through the bead again. String on two beads, then proceed according to Figure 8. For a single-bead edging, follow Figure 9.

HOW MANY BEADS WILL YOU NEED?

Bead Size	Length of Strand		
	16 in.(41 cm)	18 in.(46.5 cm)	24 in.(61.5 cm)
4mm	100	112	153
6mm	68	76	100
8mm	50	56	76
10mm	40	45	61

GLITTERING GOLD NECKLACE

A FEW STUNNING BEADS, A HANDFUL OF ACCENT BEADS, A SIMPLE DESIGN—THE
ELEMENTS OF FINE JEWELRY. THE LARGE GLASS BEADS IN THIS NECKLACE, HAND-
FORMED BY DONNA ZALUSKY, TAKE THEIR GLITTER AND TEXTURE FROM THE SILVER
FOIL INSIDE. A SIMILAR DESIGN WILL SHOWCASE YOUR FAVORITE BEADS.

1 Cut about 1 yard (.9 m) of tigertail.

2 Position a large wafer bead in the center of the
tigertail. (Starting in the center allows you to adjust
the length of the necklace to your liking.)

3 Working from the center outward, add glass and

crystal spacers as shown, or vary the pattern
according to your own taste. Continue until all nine
wafer beads are used. Finish with spacers on each
side.

4 Finish the ends with crimp beads and a sterling
silver clasp.

DESIGN:

Donna Zalusky

HOW-TO:

Crimp beads, page 15.

YOU WILL NEED

Tigertail

9 large, glass wafer
beads

Clear glass spacer
beads

Yellow crystal spacer
beads

2 crimp beads

Chain-nose pliers

Silver clasp

PRAYER BOX NECKLACE

THE FOCAL POINTS OF THIS NECKLACE ARE TWO NEPALESE PRAYER BOXES, THE SILVER ONE IN THE CENTER AND THE LAPIS LAZULI ONE ON THE RIGHT. PRAYER BOXES ARE DESIGNED TO HOLD MANTRAS FOR MEDITATION. ECHOING THE PRAYER THEME ARE TWO PERUVIAN MILAGRO CHARMS—THE COW AT LEFT AND THE HUMAN TORSO AT RIGHT—WHICH ARE PLACED ON STATUES OF SAINTS TO ACCOMPANY PRAYERS FOR HEALING.

1 Starting in the center and working out to each end, string the beads on the tigertail.

2 Finish the ends with crimp beads and add a clasp.

DESIGN:

Jana Hunt Newton

HOW-TO:

Crimp beads, page 15.

YOU WILL NEED

Tigertail

Beads and charms

Crimp beads

Chain-nose pliers

Clasp

BRACELET WITH BEADS AND CHARMS

VIRTUALLY ALL CHARMS COME WITH A LOOP ATTACHED, WHICH CAN SIMPLY BE STRUNG ONTO THE THREAD ALONG WITH THE BEADS. FOR THE OCCASIONAL CHARM WITH NO LOOP, IT'S A SIMPLE MATTER TO MAKE YOUR OWN. (SEE MAKING A WIRE LOOP, PAGE 45.)

DESIGN:

Melanie Alter

YOU WILL NEED

Strong beading thread

Beading needle

Beads, charms, and cones

2 end caps

Bead cement

Hook-and-eye clasp

1 Cut a piece of thread twice the length of the bracelet plus 8 inches (20 cm). (Standard bracelet length is 7 inches, or 18 cm.) Double the thread but don't knot it.

2 String the beads, charms, and (if desired) cones.

3 String on an end cap. Take the thread through the loop in one half of the clasp and then back through the end cap. Knot the thread twice and clip the tail. Dot the knot with bead cement and allow to dry.

4 Thread the needle onto the other end of the bracelet. Add an end cap and finish this end of the bracelet as you did the first.

A LONG STRAND FOR SPECIAL BEADS

THIS LONG NECKLACE CAN BE SLIPPED OVER THE HEAD AND WORN EITHER SINGLE OR DOUBLED. SPECIAL BEADS INCLUDE A MALACHITE PI, A SWIRL-CARVED ONYX BALL, HANDMADE SILVER FROM SRI LANKA, AND SWAROVSKI CRYSTAL.

DESIGN:

Cynthia Rutledge

HOW-TO:

Making a continuous necklace, page 20.

YOU WILL NEED

Beading thread

2 flexible beading needles

Clip or tape

Glass, stone, silver, and semiprecious beads

Seed beads, size 11

Cut beads, size 11

Bead glue

1 Cut a piece of thread twice the finished length of the necklace plus 1 yard (.9 m). For example, to make the 50-inch strand shown here, cut the thread 3-3/4 yards long (3.46 m).

2 Thread on a flexible needle. Double the thread but don't knot it. Clip or tape the tails together temporarily about 8 inches (20.5 cm) from the end.

3 String on the beads. One good approach is to create a series of segments that feature four to seven seed beads, several accent beads, and a special bead.

4 When the beads are strung, unclip the tails and string the second needle onto them. Cross-thread the necklace and knot several times on each side. Dab the knots with glue.

A GOOD BASE RECIPE FOR MIXING COLORS IS A LIGHT, A MEDIUM, A DARK, A BRIGHT, AND AN ACCENT.

CYNTHIA RUTLEDGE

COLOR BAND SEED NECKLACE

SMALL SEED BEADS DON'T HAVE TO BE WOVEN INTO INTRICATE PATTERNS. SIMPLY STRUNG ON MULTIPLE STRANDS IN THE SAME ORDER, THEY PRODUCE WONDERFUL BANDS OF COLOR.

DESIGN:

Lynn Nelson

HOW-TO:

Using cones, page 21.

YOU WILL NEED

Beading thread

Masking tape

Beading needles

Seed beads (size 10 to 13) in a variety of colors

Pair of cones

Hook-and-eye clasp

Large eye pin or 18-gauge wire

Round-nose pliers

Bead cement

1 Decide the length of the necklace and the number of strands. (The one shown is 28 inches, or 72 cm, end to end and contains 13 strands of beads.)

2 Determine the order of the color bands and how wide you want each band to be. Write down a list of how the necklace will go—for example, 10 coral, 20 teal, 3 pink, 1 gold, 3 pink, 10 coral, etc. Or, if you'd rather measure than count, 1 inch (2.5 cm) of coral, 2 inches (5 cm) of teal, etc.

3 Cut a piece of thread 6 to 8 inches (15.5 to 20.5 cm) longer than the necklace will be and tape one end to the table with masking tape. String the beads in the chosen order. Set the strand aside, taping both ends.

4 String the remaining strands of beads in the same manner.

5 Finish the necklace with the cones and clasp.

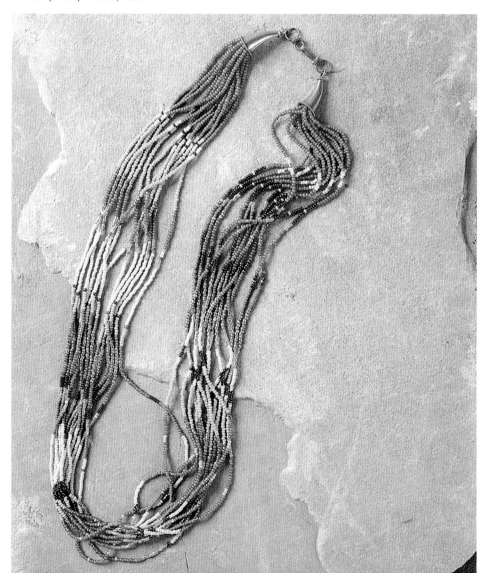

LOOPED EARRINGS

THESE ELEGANT EARRINGS ARE SIMPLY LOOPS OF BEADS TUCKED INTO A PAIR OF CONES. HERE SEED BEADS COMBINE WITH ACCENT BEADS OF GLASS, AFRICAN TURQUOISE, JASPER, AND CARNELIAN. THE FINDINGS ARE VERMEIL (GILDED SILVER).

DESIGN:

Cynthia Rutledge

HOW-TO:

Using cones, page 21.

YOU WILL NEED

Seed beads

Accent beads

Beading thread

Flexible bead needle

Round-nose pliers

Chain-nose pliers

6 inches (15.5 cm) of 20-gauge wire, cut into 2 3-inch (7.5 cm) pieces

Pair of 6mm ball posts with loop, and pair of ear nuts

Bead cement

1 Cut 10 18-inch (46 cm) pieces of bead thread.

2 Thread a flexible needle onto one of the pieces and string 3 inches of seed beads and accent beads. (Begin and end with seed beads, so that the ends of the strands will fit easily inside the cones.) Remove the needle, center the beads on the thread, and set aside.

3 String nine more strands of beads in a similar fashion.

4 With the round-nose pliers, form a small wrapped loop on one end of a piece of wire.

5 Gather five strands of beads into one bundle and fold them in half, so you are holding their tails. Lay the bundle on your work surface in a U shape. Take the left-hand threads through the loop in one direction and the right-hand threads through the loop in the opposite direction. See Figure 1. Tie all tails in a knot around the loop and apply a dab of bead cement.

6 String the other five strands on the second wire in a similar fashion. Trim thread ends close to the knot and add more cement if necessary.

7 Slide a cone onto a wire stem. See Figure 2. Pull the wire snugly into the cone, which should cover the loop and some of the seeds. Arrange the loops to your satisfaction.

8 Holding the cone with one hand, make a second loop in the wire, about 1/8 inch (.3 cm) from the top of the cone. Attach the stem loop to the post loop. Repeat for other earring.

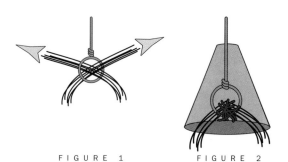

FIGURE 1   FIGURE 2

SEED BEAD NECKLACE WITH GLASS ACCENTS

IN THIS NECKLACE, TOPAZ JAPANESE MATTE SEED BEADS (WHICH SHADE TO ROSE PINK AND GRAY BLUE IN BRIGHT LIGHT) ARE INTERSPERSED WITH LARGE GLASS BEADS IN CREAMY BEIGE, GOLD, AND BLACK. THE HOMEMADE CLASP CONSISTS OF A VERY LARGE BEAD AT ONE END AND A LOOP OF 23 SEED BEADS AT THE OTHER.

DESIGN:

Gini Williams

HOW-TO:

Burying the thread,
page 63.

YOU WILL NEED

Beading thread

5 beading needles

Japanese matte seed beads, size 6

Medium and large glass accent beads

Very large glass bead (for the clasp)

Bead cement

1 Cut five pieces of bead thread at least 12 inches (31 cm) longer than you want the necklace to be. (The one shown is 28 inches, or 72 cm., long.) Tie the threads together at one end. Dot knot with bead cement. Thread a needle onto each thread at the other end.

2 Since all five strands of the necklace are about the same length, there's no need to work on a multiple-strand bead board. Simply string the beads onto the threads. If you work from one end of the necklace to the other, stringing all five strands at the same time, you'll be able to intersperse the large beads, so that they don't fall at the same places on the five strands.

3 When you're through stringing, tie the five threads together.

4 At one end, take all five threads through the very large glass bead, then through a seed bead. Make sure the glass bead is tight against the necklace and that the knot is buried in the large bead's hole. Take the threads around the seed bead, then back through the glass bead. Bury the threads in a few beads, knot the tails to the necklace, and clip the ends.

5 To make the loop at the other end, take all five threads through a medium-small accent bead, then through 23 seed beads. Bring the threads back through the pony bead, burying the knot inside the bead hole. Bury the threads in a few beads and knot the tails to the necklace. Trim the ends.

> **DON'T BE CONSTRAINED BY THE LINEAGE OF YOUR BEADS. COMBINING BEADS FROM DIFFERENT CULTURES AND TIME PERIODS CAN PRODUCE INTERESTING JEWELRY.**
>
> **ERIN EVERETT**

BLACK AND WHITE CHOKER

THIS HANDSOME CHOKER CONSISTS OF WIRED BEADS STRUNG BETWEEN TWO PIECES OF LEATHER CORD.

DESIGN:

Lonnie Lovness

HOW-TO:

Making a wire loop, page 45; jump rings, page 14.

YOU WILL NEED

28-gauge brass wire

Round-nose pliers

18 black 9mm beads

16 white 9mm beads

2 hexagonal brass beads with large holes

Assorted glass, ceramic, brass, polymer, and bone beads

4 feet (1.2 m) of 2mm round leather cord

2 brass cord-end caps

Bead cement

1 The choker shown is about 6 inches (15.5 cm) long and 1-1/2 inches (4 cm) wide. It has 18 cross pieces of wired beads. For a longer choker, add more wired beads.

2 First, make the cross pieces. Cut 18 pieces of wire about 2 inches (5 cm) long. Make a loop in one end of each wire, string on about 3/4 inch (2 cm) of beads, and make a loop in the other end. Make sure the cross pieces are the same length, but mix up the beads, including some long beads and some rows of short ones.

3 Arrange the cross pieces in the desired order for the choker. Intersperse pieces that feature a long bead with pieces composed of several small beads.

4 Cut a 24-inch (61.5 cm) piece of leather cord. Thread it through a wire loop of the first cross piece, then through a black pony bead. Now thread it through the loop of the second cross piece, then through a white pony bead. Continue to alternate cross pieces with black and white pony beads until all cross pieces are strung. End with a black bead.

5 Cut another 24-inch piece of cord and thread it alternately through the other ends of the cross pieces and through black and white pony beads, beginning and ending with black beads.

6 At each end of the choker, bring the two cords together. Take both cords through a large-holed bead and loop them into a single overhand knot.

7 Try on the choker for length and trim the ends of the cord evenly. Coat the ends of the cords heavily with glue and insert them into the cord-ends. Allow to dry. Attach a jump ring to each end. Add a hook to one end and a chain to the other. If desired, finish the end of the chain with a bead or two on a short head pin.

BEADS OF BONE
AND HORN

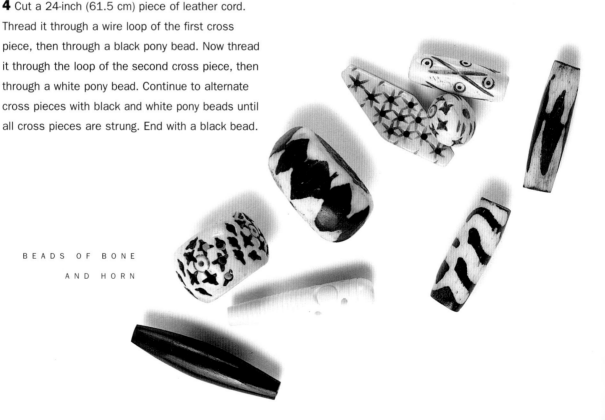

AFRICAN NECKLACE

THE CARVED BONE PENDANTS ON THIS NECKLACE ARE FROM ETHIOPIA. SET OFF WITH RESIN BEADS, BRASS HEISHI, AND BRONZE CONES, THEY MAKE A STRIKING NECKLACE.

DESIGN:

Melanie Alter

HOW-TO:

Using cones, page 21; making a wire loop, page 45.

YOU WILL NEED

3 bone pendants

Wire cutters

22-gauge wire

Round-nose pliers

Chain-nose pliers

Beading thread

Beading needles

Twisted-wire needle

Resin beads

Brass heishi

Bead cement

5 brass cones

Hook-and-eye clasp

1 First wire the pendants so they can be strung onto the necklace. Cut a piece of wire about 6 inches (15.5 cm) long and take it through a pendant. Then, using the pliers, wrap the wire around itself just above the pendant, creating a loop. Clip the short tail. Take the wire through the cone, push the cone down to cover the first loop, and make a loop above the cone. Clip the tail. Turn the loop so it points front to back, allowing the pendant to hang correctly. Repeat with remaining pendants.

2 Thread three needles with beading thread and double each strand. String the three strands of the necklace, positioning each pendant near the center. Place brass heishi between all the resin beads, varying the number of heishi at will.

3 Remove the needles from the thread. On each side of the necklace, tie the six threads into a square knot. Dot with bead glue and allow to dry.

4 Take all six threads through a twisted-wire needle. Treating the six threads as one, string on a cone and the remaining beads.

5 On each side of the necklace, take the threads through the loop in one side of the clasp. Take the thread back through a few beads, knot it, and dab it with bead glue.

BEADS OF BRASS AND IRON.

TOLKIEN EARRINGS

NAMED FOR J. R. TOLKIEN'S *LORD OF THE RINGS*, THESE EARRINGS ARE SIMPLY STRANDS OF BEADS LOOPED AROUND A RING.

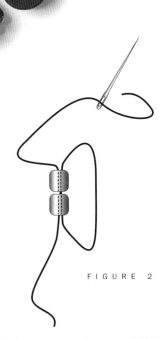

DESIGN:

Cheri Lynn Waltz

HOW-TO:

Making fringe, page 22; making a wire loop, page 45.

YOU WILL NEED

2 small doughnuts (or rings)

10 hex-cut seed beads

Bead thread

Beading needle

Seed beads, size 11

Small crystal, glass, metal, and/or semi-precious beads

2 ear posts with balls

2 head pins

Round-nose pliers

1 Pick up two hex beads on your needle. See Figure 1. Push them down almost to the end of your thread, leaving a 7-inch (18 cm) tail.

2 Bring the needle back through the two hex beads, moving in the same direction. See Figure 2.

3 Pull the top hex bead around so the beads are side by side. See Figure 3.

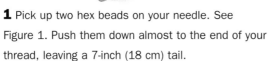

FIGURE 1

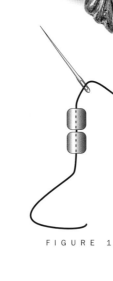

FIGURE 2

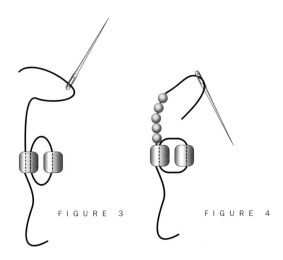

FIGURE 3   FIGURE 4

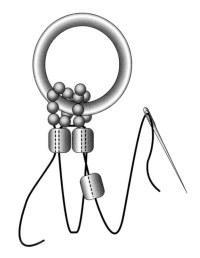

FIGURE 5

4 Bring the needle up through the first hex bead again. Add enough seed beads to go around the ring without leaving any thread showing. See Figure 4. Count the number of seed beads.

5 Wrap the row of seed beads around the ring. Bring the needle down through the first hex bead and up through the second hex bead. See Figure 5.

6 String on the same number of seed beads. Go through the ring and down through the second hex bead. Pick up another hex bead. See Figure 5.

7 Anchor the new hex bead to its neighbor by going down through the previous hex bead and up through the one you just added. See Figure 6. String the same number of seed beads, go through the ring, and down the hex bead.

8 Repeat until you have five loops of seed beads going around the ring.

9 Add five strands of fringe, anchoring it in the hex beads. See Figure 7.

10 Run a head pin up through the top of the ring. Add a bead, form the head pin into a loop, and attach the loop to the ear post. Repeat with other earring.

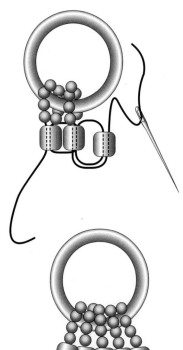

FIGURE 6

FIGURE 7

AMETHYST AND ROSE QUARTZ NECKLACE

TURQUOISE, AMETHYST, AND ROSE QUARTZ BEADS ALTERNATE WITH
HAND-CARVED PURPLE FETISHES AND SILVER CHARMS TO PRODUCE
A STRIKING NECKLACE.

1 Lay out the lower portion of the necklace on the bead board (or on a towel, if you don't have a board).

2 Cut three pieces of tigertail, each the length of one entire strand plus 10 inches (25.5 cm). The extra is for last-minute changes of heart.

3 Wrap tape around one end of a piece of tigertail, to keep the beads from falling off. String the beads and charms for the lower part of the necklace, and tape the other end. Repeat with the other two strands.

4 Remove the tape and add a three-hole spacer at each end. String the heishi on the upper strands. Add the crimp beads and the clasp.

DESIGN:

Lynn Nelson

HOW-TO:

Split rings, page 14;
crimp beads, page 15.

YOU WILL NEED

Multistrand bead board (optional)

Semiprecious and glass beads, chips, charms

Heishi

Masking tape

Tigertail

Split rings

2 3-hole spacers

Hook-and-eye clasp for 3-strand necklace

12 crimp beads

Chain-nose pliers

BEADED WATCH BAND

TWO CHINESE ENAMEL BEADS (FLEA MARKET FINDS) BECAME THE
FOCAL POINTS OF THIS WATCH BAND, THEIR VIBRANT COLORS
ECHOED BY GLASS BEADS.

1 Measure your wrist; measure the width of the watch component. Subtract the watch measurement from your wrist measurement and divide by two; this is the length of each side of the watch band. Don't make it too tight; the finished piece should fit like a bracelet.

2 Cut six pieces of tigertail 4 inches (10.5 cm) longer than the length of each side of the band. Loop a piece around one of the bars of the watch face, slide a crimp bead up until it covers both sides of the loop, and squeeze it closed with the pliers. Repeat with remaining tigertail, so that you have three pieces on each side of the watch.

3 String beads on the three wires on one side of the watch, stopping about 1/2 inch (1.5 cm) short of your band measurement.

4 If desired, treat some of the beads as charms. Thread a bead cap on a head pin, then add a bead. Make a loop above the bead and string the loop on the wire.

5 Take all three pieces of tigertail through one large-holed bead, then through a crimp bead. Loop them through a hook-and-eye clasp, then take them back through the crimp bead and the large-holed bead. Squeeze the crimp bead closed. Take each of the wire strands through another bead or two and clip the tails.

6 Repeat for other side of watch.

DESIGN:

Margaret Reed

HOW-TO:

*Crimp beads, page 15;
making a wire loop,
page 45.*

YOU WILL NEED

Watch face

Tape measure

Tigertail

Crimp beads

Chain-nose pliers

Beads

Head pins and bead
caps (optional)

MULTISTRAND NECKLACE

BONE SPACERS LET THIS COLORFUL NECKLACE GO FROM ONE STRAND TO FIVE, THEN BACK AGAIN.

DESIGN:

Galen Madaras

YOU WILL NEED

Tigertail

Clasp

2 2-hole spacers

2 4-hole spacers

2 5-hole spacers

Assorted beads

Clasp

1 Lay out your beads until you're pleased with the order. You'll be stringing from the right end of the necklace to the left end.

2 Cut three 60-inch (154 cm) pieces of tigertail.

3 Fold the pieces of tigertail in half. Take the folded centers through the loop on one piece of the clasp. Take each pair of tail ends through its respective fold and pull snugly. See Figure 1. You will have six strands of tigertail to work with.

FIGURE 1

4 Treating all six strands as one, string on a bone pipe bead, a scull, and an African love bead.

5 Separate the tigertail into two strands. String a pipe bead onto each strand, then add the two-hole spacer. String two African sand beads onto each strand.

6 Separate each strand in half again and take the four strands through a four-hole spacer.

7 Separate the tigertail into five strands. (You'll have one extra piece; double up for the bottom strand of beads, which will carry the most weight.) String a small bone bead on each strand, then add the five-bead spacer.

8 String the first (and shortest) strand of beads. As shown, it is 9-1/2 inches (24.5 cm) long. It consists largely of turquoise chips with a bauxite pipe stone in the center.

9 The second strand, about 11 inches (28 cm) long, consists of small African glass beads.

10 String the third strand, which consists of lapis lazuli chips, Venetian glass beads, then the fourth, which has beads of bone and semiprecious stones (with 10 blue African snake beads in the center).

11 The fifth strand combines African glass, silver charms, bone, turquoise, and glass, with an African turquoise turtle settled firmly into the center.

12 Check to see that the five strands "nest" comfortably. String the left side of the necklace, making it a mirror image of the right.

13 Thread the tigertail around the other half of the clasp and tie two double knots. Cut the ends to about 2 inches (5 cm) and feed the tails back into the beads.

WORKING WITH WIRE

WIRE ADDS A DISTINCTIVE DESIGN ELEMENT TO BEAD JEWELRY. IT'S AVAILABLE AT BEAD SHOPS AND CRAFT STORES IN A MARVELOUS ARRAY OF METALS. STERLING SILVER, COPPER, AND GOLD-FILLED ARE PERHAPS THE BEST KNOWN, BUT OTHERS DESERVE A LOOK. ANNEALED STEEL IS BOLD AND BLACK. DISTINCTIVE AND CONTEMPORARY, NIOBIUM BOASTS BRILLIANT COLORS, CREATED WHEN AN ELECTRIC CURRENT IS PASSED THROUGH THE MATERIAL. ALSO AVAILABLE ARE VARIOUS "BASE" METALS—GOOD FOR A WEAR-ONCE PAIR OF EARRINGS AND EXCELLENT FOR PRACTICING NEW TECHNIQUES.

DESIGN:

Kimberley Adams.

> MATCH THE QUALITY OF THE WIRE AND THE FINDINGS WITH THE QUALITY OF THE BEADS.
> **KIMBERLEY ADAMS**

THESE HAND-WORKED GLASS BEADS NEED LITTLE ELSE IN THE WAY OF DECORATION. THEY'RE SIMPLY STRUNG ON RATTAIL. NOTE THE WIRE LOOP ABOVE EACH BEAD AND THE WIRE SPIRAL BELOW.

GAUGES

Wire is sold in various thickness, or *gauges*. The higher the number, the thinner the wire. Fine and flexible 24-gauge wire is useful for small beads with small holes. Thicker 20-gauge wire is strong enough to wire beads together for dangles and drop earrings. Tougher 18-gauge is rigid enough to hold its shape once it's bent into graceful curves.

TOOLS

In addition to the basic jewelry-making tools described on page 12—wire cutters, round-nose pliers, and chain-nose pliers—you'll need the following.

Hammer and anvil. Wire that's hammered flat acquires a whole new (and very classy) look. An ordinary household hammer will work fine; a ball peen hammer (the kind with the round knob opposite the hitting surface) adds more weight and thus force. An anvil is handy. To hammer metal flat, you need a flat working surface that won't yield or chip. In lieu of an anvil, look around the house for other metal items that will fill the bill.

File. Necessary for putting a sharp point on the end of a wire pin.

MAKING A WIRE LOOP

Once you know how to do this, you can make most of the projects in this chapter.

1 Using chain-nose pliers, bend the wire into a right angle. If you're working with wired beads (on a head pin, for example), leave enough room above the top bead for two or three wraps of wire. See Figure 1.

2 With the round-nose pliers, grasp the wire close

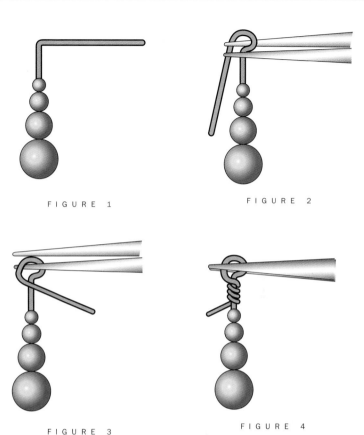

FIGURE 1

FIGURE 2

FIGURE 3

FIGURE 4

to the right-angle bend. With your other hand, wrap the wire around the top jaw of the pliers. See Figure 2.

3 Remove the pliers, then reinsert them with the lower jaw inside the loop. Again, using the other hand, wrap the wire around the pliers. See Figure 3. If the loop is off center, use the pliers to bend it upright.

4 Hold the loop firmly with your chain-nose pliers. With your other hand, wrap the wire around the neck of the loop until you are almost to the top bead, keeping the wire at a right angle as you wrap it. See Figure 4.

5 Cut the wire end as closely as possible and tuck the end into the remaining space.

DESIGN:

Pat Poole-Frank

MAKING A WIRE SPIRAL

The spiral is a classy way to keep a bead from falling off the bottom of a wire.

1 Using round-nose pliers, form a loop in the bottom of the wire.

2 Using chain-nose pliers, grasp the loop across its flat surface. Turn the loop sideways, creating a spiral. See Figure 5.

QUICK DROP EARRINGS

For instant earrings, you need only beads, head pins, and findings.

First string a few beads on a head pin (or on several head pins). Now check the loops on the findings.

FIGURE 5

If they can be opened, twist them open. Finish wrapping and closing the loops on the head pins, slip them into the earring loop, and close it.

If the loops on the findings are soldered shut, make the first bend for the head pin loop. See Figure 3 (page 45). Slide the finding's loop along the wire end until it snaps into the half-formed loop. Now finish wrapping the head pin loop.

GLASS BEADS AND SILVER CHAIN

THESE STUNNING NECKLACES COMBINE HAND-WORKED GLASS BEADS, STERLING SILVER WIRE, AND LENGTHS OF PURCHASED CHAIN. EARRINGS COMPLETE THE SET.

DESIGN:

Kimberley Adams

HOW-TO:

Making a wire loop, page 45; making a wire spiral, page 46.

YOU WILL NEED

Large focal beads

Smaller accent beads

Wire cutters

20-gauge sterling silver wire

Round-nose pliers

Chain-nose pliers

Purchased sterling silver chain

Pair of ear wires

1 The basic unit of the necklace is a large focal bead with one or two small accent beads on each side of it—all threaded on a piece of wire, with loops on each end holding the beads in place. These basic bead units are joined in groups of three. In turn, the groups are connected with chain.

2 Lay out your beads until you're pleased with the order. To avoid reopening and closing a lot of loops, work from one end of the necklace to the other.

3 Cut a piece of wire to a convenient working length—say, 8 inches (20.5 cm). (You'll soon discover what length works for you; you want it long enough to handle easily but not so long that you waste a lot of sterling wire.)

4 Form a loop in one end of the wire. Thread on one or two small accent beads, a large focal bead, and one or two more accent beads. Form a loop in the other end of the wire and clip the excess.

5 Thread a second piece of wire through a loop of the first completed segment; form the new wire into a loop. Thread on the beads of your second unit and form a loop in the other end.

6 Repeat Step 5 with your third group of beads, but don't make the last loop. See Figure 1. You should now have three wired units of beads.

7 With the wire cutters, cut a piece of chain about 1-1/2 inches (4 cm) long. Make sure you have com-

FIGURE 2

plete links. Thread the chain onto the wired beads and form the wire into a loop. See Figure 2.

8 At the other end of the chain, attach a working length of wire and form a loop. Thread on three beads.

9 Continue around the necklace until it is completed, connecting the last two loops to each other.

10 Check carefully for burrs, squeezing the ends into the coils as necessary.

11 For the red earrings, cut a 6-inch (15.5 cm) piece of wire and form a loop in one end. Add accent beads and a focal bead, form a loop in the wire's other end, and attach it to the ear wire. Repeat for other earring.

12 For the lavender earrings, cut a 6-inch piece of wire and form a spiral in one end. String on a bead, then form a wire loop at the other end. Wire the larger bead and attach it to the smaller one. Add the ear wire. Repeat with other earring.

FIGURE 1

MASAI BRACELET

UNLIKE A BRACELET STRUNG ON SPIRALING MEMORY WIRE, THE STRANDS OF THIS BRACELET REMAIN FIXED AND PARALLEL. THE BRILLIANT BEADS ARE AFRICAN.

DESIGN:

Leslie Bruntsch

HOW-TO:

Making a wire loop, page 45.

YOU WILL NEED

3 feet (92.5 cm) of 18-gauge sterling silver wire

Wire cutters

Assorted beads

Chain-nose pliers

Round-nose pliers

2 sterling silver 3-hole spacers

1 Cut three pieces of wire 9 inches (23 cm) long.

2 With the round-nose pliers, make a loop at one end of each wire.

3 String the beads on the wires, placing the spacers one-third and two-thirds of the way around the bracelet.

4 Make a wire loop at the other end of each wire.

5 To make the clasp, cut two 4-inch (10.5 cm) pieces of wire. Using the chain-nose pliers, bend each wire into a triangle with 1/2-inch (1.5 cm) sides. Finish one triangle with a loop. Make a loop in the other triangle and finish with a hook. Attach the two parts of the clasp to the loops of the bracelet.

HOOP EARRINGS

WHILE HOOP EARRINGS ARE WIDELY AVAILABLE, IT'S FUN (AND OFTEN CONVENIENT) TO MAKE YOUR OWN, SO THAT THE WIRE IN THE FOCAL BEADS AND THE WIRE IN THE HOOPS CAN MATCH EXACTLY.

1 To wire a focal bead, cut a piece of wire about 6 inches (15.5 cm) long. Make a spiral in one end. Add the focal bead, an accent bead or two, and finish with a closed loop on top. Repeat for other earring.

2 For the hoop, cut a 4-inch (10.5 cm) piece of wire. Make a small loop at one end, using the round-nose pliers.

3 From the other end, string on four accent beads, the focal bead, then four more accent beads.

4 With the chain-nose pliers, bend the other end of the wire at a right angle. To close the earring, hook the bent end into the loop.

DESIGN:

Kimberley Adams

HOW-TO:

Making a wire loop, page 45; making a wire spiral, page 46.

YOU WILL NEED

Wire cutters
20-gauge gold wire
Round-nose pliers
Chain-nose pliers
Pair of focal beads
Small accent beads

FLUORITE AND AMETHYST NECKLACE

THIS SUBTLE NECKLACE TAKES A FIRST STEP INTO WIREWORK. WHILE
THE BEADS ARE STRUNG ON BEADING THREAD, THEY ARE SET OFF BY
HANDMADE WIRE COILS AND A HANDSOMELY WIRED DOUGHNUT.

DESIGN:

Erin Everett

HOW-TO:

*Using bead tips,
page 15.*

YOU WILL NEED

Chain-nose pliers

Round-nose pliers

Awl

Wire cutters

22-gauge sterling silver
wire

20-gauge sterling silver
wire

Hammer

Anvil or bench block

Fluorite doughnut

Fluorite beads and
chips

Amethyst chips

Beading thread

Beading needle

Bead tips

Jump rings

Hook-and-eye clasp

1 To make the wire coils, wrap 22-gauge wire around the awl, gripping the wire securely with the chain-nose pliers. Remove the coiled wire from the awl and cut it after every five coils. Set aside.

2 Now wrap the doughnut. Cut a piece of 20-gauge wire 8 to 10 inches (20.5-25.5 cm) long. Measure the distance across half the doughnut. Using the round-nose pliers, form some interesting curves about one-third of the way down the wire. Hold the curved portion against the doughnut, to make sure it fits.

3 Gripping one end of the wire with the pliers, lay the curved portion on the anvil and hammer it flat where it will cross the doughnut.

4 Take the wire through the center of the doughnut and twist the two ends around each other, right next to the doughnut. Clip one wire end close to the twisted section. Using round-nose pliers, form a loop in the remaining wire. Clip excess. See Figure 1. Clip the wire ends. Make sure the loop goes front to back.

5 Lay out the beads in the order they'll be strung, making sure the two sides will be symmetrical.

6 Thread the needle, double the thread, and knot it. Add a bead tip, then string the beads, chips, wire coils, and doughnut. Add a bead tip to the other end, then finish the necklace with jump rings and a clasp.

FIGURE 1

BEADS FROM SEMIPRECIOUS STONES AND CORAL

TURQUOISE NECKLACE WITH YIN-YANG BEADS

IN THIS DESIGN, THE GRACEFUL CURVES OF SILVER WIRE ARE AS IMPORTANT AS THE BEADS.

DESIGN:

Galen Madaras

HOW-TO:

Making a wire loop, page 45.

YOU WILL NEED

Large turquoise dough-nut, 2 small turquoise doughnuts, turquoise chips, yin-yang beads, black accent beads

18- and 20-gauge ster-ling silver wire

Anvil

Hammer

Wire cutters

Chain-nose pliers

Round-nose pliers

1 Arrange the beads in an order that pleases you.

2 To wire the large doughnut, first cut a 4-inch (10.5 cm) length of 18-gauge wire. Measure 2 inch-es (5 cm) down the wire. Place the wire on the anvil and hammer 1 inch (2.5 cm) of wire below that, until it is as flat as you want it.

3 Thread the wire stem through the doughnut, with the 2-inch section on top. The flattened section should cross the doughnut. Bring the back wire up behind the doughnut and wrap it around the stem two full turns. Trim the excess wrapped wire and squeeze the cut end into the wrap with the chain-nose pliers.

4 String a turquoise chip, a yin-yang bead, and a second chip on the wire stem. Make a loop in the top of the stem and trim the wire end.

5 To create the zigzag wire holding the doughnut, cut a 7-inch (18 cm) piece of 18-gauge wire. Grasp the center of the wire with the round-nose pliers and use your other hand to bend each end up around the pliers, creating a V shape. About 3/4 inch (2 cm) from the center of the V, grasp the wire

again and bend the wire back down about 1/4 inch (1 cm). Continue in a similar fashion until you have a number of bends on each side of the center V. String a turquoise chip on one side of the wire.

6 Thread the turquoise doughnut onto the center wire and form loops in each end of the wire. Place the centerpiece wire on the anvil and carefully ham-mer it as flat as desired.

7 Cut a 3-inch (7.5 cm) stem of 20-gauge wire. Make a loop at one end and string on three turquoise chips. Make a loop in the other end, attaching it to the centerpiece wire before closing the loop completely. Repeat for other side of neck-lace.

8 Cut a 4-inch (10.5 cm) stem and make a loop in one end. Add a curve to the wire as you did to the centerpiece and flatten it as before. String on the beads and attach the segment to the previous one. Repeat for other side.

9 Continue around the necklace, creating wire seg-ments of beads and looping them to each other. Attach a clasp at the back.

SPIRAL WIRE BRACELET

THANKS TO WIDELY AVAILABLE "MEMORY WIRE"—STEEL WIRE THAT REMAINS
COILED—THERE IS NO EASIER JEWELRY TO MAKE.

1 Cut the wire to the length desired, depending on
the number of coils you want in the bracelet.

2 String the beads onto the wire. Avoid beads with
small holes—if you have to force one around the
wire, use another bead—and avoid very long beads,
which will distort the wire's curves.

3 Check that the beads lie next to each other well.
Avoid large beads on adjacent coils that crowd each
other and force the coils apart.

4 Form a loop in each end of the wire, to hold the
beads. If desired, hang a charm from each loop.

DESIGN:

Jana Hunt Newton

HOW-TO:

Making a wire loop,
page 45.

YOU WILL NEED

Memory wire

Heavy-duty wire cutters

Sturdy round-
nose pliers

Large-holed beads

Charms (optional)

PIN WITH DANGLES

GIANT SAFETY PINS WITH BUILT-IN LOOPS ARE AVAILABLE WHEREVER JEWELRY FINDINGS ARE SOLD.

1 With the 20-gauge wire, make as many dangles as there are loops in the pin, working from the bottom to the top of each dangle and including two wired segments in each one. The dangles should be about the same length; if some beads are squatty, add an extra small bead to even out the lengths.

2 Attach the dangles to the loops in the pin. If desired, open the loops enough to add some seed beads to the pin itself.

DESIGN:

Kimberley Adams

HOW-TO:

Making a wire loop, page 45; making a wire spiral, page 46

YOU WILL NEED

20-gauge silver wire

Purchased decorative pin

Round-nose pliers

Chain-nose pliers

Seed beads, size 6

Large beads in various shapes

TURQUOISE EARRINGS WITH GOLD WIRE

THESE STUNNING EARRINGS DEMONSTRATE JUST HOW INTERESTING A SINGLE COLOR FAMILY CAN BE.

DESIGN:

Jana Hunt Newton

HOW-TO:

Making a wire loop, page 45; making a wire spiral, page 46.

YOU WILL NEED

2 turquoise cabochons (large, oval stones that are flat on one side)

Rotary hand-held carving tool or diamond file

22-gauge gold-filled wire

Round-nose pliers

Chain-nose pliers

Beads of turquoise, glass, and crystal

Ear posts with gold balls

1 Around each cabochon, carve a groove to hold the wire that will encircle it. The best tool for this is a rotary, hand-held power tool; use its slit-carver bit. You can also use a diamond file, if you have one. In the absence of either tool, find a friendly jeweler who will carve two grooves for a nominal fee.

2 To encircle a "cab" with wire, first cut a piece of wire about 12 inches (31 cm) long. With the round-nose pliers, form a loop in the center of the wire, giving it only one twist; this will be the center loop underneath the cab. Form enough loops on each side of the center one to span the bottom of the cabochon. (In this case, nine loops were needed.) Twist each loop once.

3 Fit the looped wire into the groove at the bottom of the cabochon. Take the wire up around the left side of the cab and make a loop at the top left corner. Take the wire across the top and make a loop at the top right corner. Twist the wire ends together and clip the ends as closely as possible.

4 Using chain-nose pliers, go around the cabochon, twisting the loops a second time, tightening the wire into the grooves on the cab. Straighten the loops as necessary, positioning them evenly. Encircle the other cabochon in a similar fashion.

5 Create a dangle for each loop, using wire loops and double spirals. The dangles should grow longer as they near the center. Wire the tops as shown in the photo and attach them to the loop of the ear post.

HAIRPINS

A FEW BOLD BEADS AND A PIECE OF WIRE CAN PRODUCE AN ARRESTING HAIRPIN.

1 Cut a piece of wire about 18 inches (46 cm) long.

2 Starting about 7 inches (18 cm) from one end of the wire, use the pliers to make turns, curves, and loops in the wire, adding beads as desired. To hold the beads in place, either make a sharp turn in the wire or flatten it just below the bead.

3 Cut the other end of the wire so that the ends of the legs are approximately even.

4 The prongs of the hairpin can be left round, but they're quite striking when they've been hammered flat. Lay the wire flat on the anvil and hammer it to about half its rounded thickness. (Be careful not to hit the beads.) Using the metal file, smooth and round the ends.

DESIGN:

Virginia Wayne

YOU WILL NEED

Wire cutters

16- or 18-gauge copper wire

Sturdy round-nose pliers

Assorted large-holed beads

Hammer and anvil (optional)

Fine metal file

STICK PIN

IF YOU STRING A BEAD ON HEAVY-GAUGE WIRE, HAMMER BOTH ENDS OF THE WIRE FLAT TO HOLD THE BEAD IN PLACE, THEN WRAP THE BEAD WITH FINER-GAUGE WIRE, YOU CAN CREATE AN ENDLESS NUMBER OF PATTERNS.

DESIGN:

Virginia Wayne

HOW-TO:

*Making a wire loop,
page 45.*

YOU WILL NEED

Wire cutters

4- to 6-inch (10.5-15.5 cm) length of 16-gauge sterling silver wire (for the stem)

12-inch (31 cm) length of 20-gauge sterling wire (for the wrapping)

Hammer

Anvil

Large-holed bead

Round-nose pliers

Metal file

1 Lay the piece of 16-gauge wire flat on the anvil and hammer one end of it relatively flat, to about half the wire's original thickness. The flattened area will extend above the bead. A flat area between 1/2 and 1-1/2 inches (1.5 to 4 cm) works well.

2 String the bead on the wire, pushing it up against the flattened section.

3 Use the pliers to make a decorative loop in the center of the 20-gauge wire. Hold the loop against the bead, to check that the size and shape are reasonable. Lay the wire loop on the anvil and hammer it flat.

4 Place the loop against the bead. Wrap one end of the wire around the stem right above the bead. Wrap the other end around the stem right below the bead. Make an interesting zigzag in the end of the tail.

5 Lay the stickpin on the anvil. Gently flatten the zigzagged tail and the stem below the wrapped bead.

6 Use the file to grind the bottom of the pin to a point.

WEAVING BASICS

THE FIRST TIME YOU TRY OFF-LOOM WEAVING, THE BEADS WILL SEEM THE SIZE OF DUST MOTES. YOUR FINGERS WILL TURN TO BRATWURST. THE THREAD WILL EXPLODE INTO TANGLED CATASTROPHE.

THE SECOND TIME WILL BE BETTER.

THE THIRD TIME—IF THERE IS A THIRD TIME—YOU'LL BE HOOKED FOR LIFE.

ENCOURAGING WORDS

Never let bead thread smell your fear. Approach it as you would a rottweiler: calmly, kindly, but with absolute assurance that you are in charge.

Directions for beadwork are more laborious than the beadwork itself. Try not to be put off by instructions that run to several paragraphs. Thread a needle, pile up some beads in your favorite colors, and start with Step 1. You'll soon be muttering, "Oh, is *that* all?"

When in doubt, keep going. Often the stitch will clearly emerge only after several rows. Weave eight or 10 rows before you throw the sample across the room.

Beads have holes. This means that you can get from any point on your weaving to any other point without leaving telltale tracks: you simply sneak from hole to hole. If you're prone to losing your way, large-holed beads are a blessing. They allow more passes of the thread. Think of them as interstates.

BEADS

Off-loom weaving is done with seed beads in various sizes. Most common is size 11. (See Seed Beads, page 9.)

THREAD

Most bead weavers work with bonded nylon, multifilament thread. It comes on large and small spools in a variety of colors, and any store with beading supplies will carry it.

The length of the working thread is a trade-off. The longer it is, the less often you have to thread a needle, but the more easily it tangles.

Some beaders double the thread to provide extra strength and security. Others work with a single thread, convinced that no amount of security is worth dealing with one more strand.

WAX

Bead thread has more body and fewer kinks if it's waxed. Before starting to weave, pull the thread over a small piece of beeswax (available at most craft stores).

NEEDLES

You'll need the rigid needles that resemble sewing "sharps." Use the largest-eyed needle your beads will put up with. The size of the bead is less important than the size of the hole. Japanese matte seed beads are universally loved, not just for their magnificent finishes, but for their huge holes. While delica beads—the tiny, cylindrical beads—look heartbreakingly small, their holes are large, allowing for larger needles.

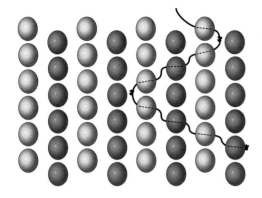

FIGURE 1

BURYING THE THREAD

Each time you begin or end a thread, you'll have a tail that must be buried in the weaving. You can bury the tails as they crop up or go back and bury them all when you've finished weaving.

To bury a tail, simply take the needle through several beads in the woven area, moving in a zigzag pattern and tying a single knot around a woven thread each time you reverse direction. See Figure 1. Clip the tail end. Seal each knot with clear nail polish or bead cement applied with a straight pin, to ensure a minute amount.

When you add a new thread, leave a 6-inch (15.5 cm) tail to bury in the future. When you're ready, thread a needle onto the tail and bury it.

ATTACHING FRINGE

Whether attached to a plastic ring or a peyote pouch, fringe is made the same way. (See Making Fringe, page 22.) Attaching it to woven jewelry is a simple matter.

If it's convenient, leave a very long tail when you first begin to weave the piece. You can use it later to make fringe. (See Comanche Earrings, page 98.) Otherwise, simply bury a new thread, exiting where you want to begin the fringe.

Essentially, exit a bead on the bottom of your piece, make a strand of fringe, then take the thread back up through the adjacent bead. The next strand of fringe can hang right next to the first one, or you can needle through several beads, adding the next strand of fringe several beads away. See Figure 2.

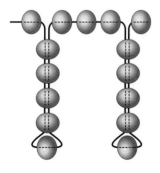

From Backstitch

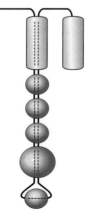

From Comanche

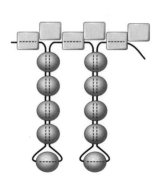

From Peyote

FIGURE 2

THE STITCHES

Each of these stitches appears in several projects. The easiest way to learn them is to weave a sample with the stitch. Once you're comfortable with it, move on to the project itself. To help visualize the stitch, many of the instructions specify light and dark beads.

BACKSTITCH

Not everyone would agree that stitching beads onto a leather backing comes under the heading of weaving. But bead embroidery, as it's often called, is a good place to get comfortable with a needle and small beads. Heavy fabric can substitute for leather in this sample.

1 Thread a beading needle with about 1 yard (.9 m) of beading thread. Double the thread and knot it.

2 Moving from wrong side to right, bring the needle up through the leather. Pick up four beads on the needle. Pull the beads down to the end of the thread and position the line of beads where you want it.

3 Insert the needle back down through the leather right next to the fourth bead.

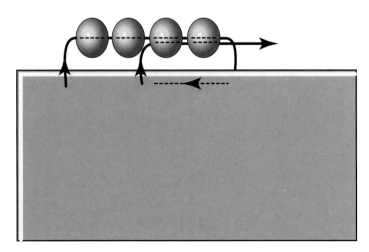

FIGURE 3

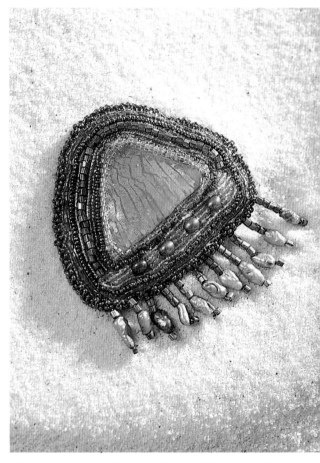

TIFFANY GLASS WITH SEED BEADS BACKSTITCHED AROUND IT.

DESIGN: GINI WILLIAMS

4 Bring the needle back up through the leather between the second and third beads. Take the needle back through the last two beads, moving in the same direction. See Figure 3.

5 Pick up four more beads and continue in the same manner.

You may want to add more than four beads at a time if you're covering a long, straight row. If the curve is sharp, you may need to add fewer. But the principle remains the same.

PEYOTE

In all its various forms, peyote is probably the most popular stitch among contemporary beaders.

Most books recommend that beginners learn the stitch using large (size 6) seed beads, and thousands have done exactly that. On the other hand, many beginners find it much easier to learn on cylinder beads, and small cylinder beads at that—commonly called delica or antique beads. They simply pop into place.

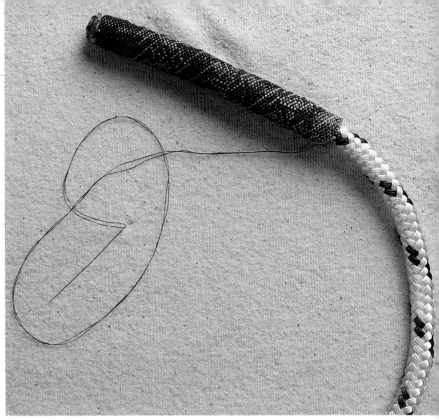

TUBULAR PEYOTE ON A POLYESTER ROPE

Tubular Peyote

This is the original peyote stitch (also called gourd stitch, Mohawk stitch, and Ute stitch). Worked over a solid, tubular core, it was used extensively to cover handles of gourd rattles for peyote ceremonies. The tube can be anything round—a pencil, a dowel, a jar, even a toilet paper tube—and can vary markedly in diameter.

The tubular peyote projects in this book use two types of cores. The slender, supple necklace on page 92 is woven around a piece of braided, polyester performance rope 1/4 inch (1 cm) in diameter. The peyote pouches on pages 86, 88, 90, and 91 were woven around the cardboard tube from a roll of paper towels or toilet tissue.

Cardboard tubes are useful for larger projects. They're lightweight and somewhat adjustable in diameter. You'll begin each project by stringing some beads and tying them in a circle. To use the

TUBULAR PEYOTE ON A CARDBOARD TUBE FROM PAPER TOWELS.

cardboard tube, first cut it down one side, from one end to the other. Overlap the cut edges and squeeze the tube to make it smaller. Insert it into the circle of beads, allowing it to expand until it is snug against them. Remove the tube long enough to tape it along the cut edges—keeping it the same size—then reinsert it into the beads.

FIGURE 4

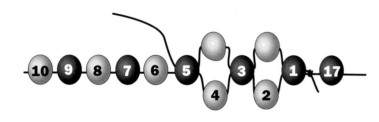

FIGURE 5

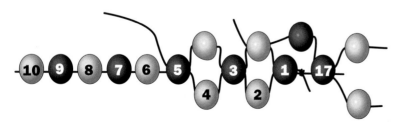

FIGURE 6

The sample projects below use both cores: rope for odd count and cardboard for even count. Either stitch will work on either tube.

TUBULAR PEYOTE, ODD COUNT
In odd-count peyote, the beads spiral continuously down the tube.

1 Thread a stiff beading needle with about 1 yard (.9 m) of thread. Do not knot it.

2 Alternating dark and light beads, string on enough beads to encircle the rope, making sure that you have an odd number of beads. Cheat on the tension if you have to. See Figure 4.

3 Tie the beads around the rope, using an over-hand knot.

4 Working right to left, take the needle through the bead to the left of the knot—bead #1. Pick up a light bead and take the needle through bead #3. Pick up another light bead and take the needle through bead #5. See Figure 5. Continue around the circle, picking up a light bead and taking the needle through every other bead (you'll always be needling through dark beads) until you're back to the beginning. The last bead you go through will be #17.

5 Now pick up a dark bead and take the needle through the closest "high bead"—a light bead that is sticking up. See Figure 6. Continue around the rope, picking up a dark bead and taking the needle through the next high (light) bead. The beads should snap into place.

6 Continue to pick up a bead and go through the next high bead. You will spiral down the rope. If you

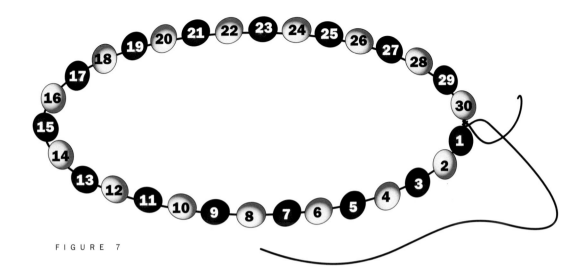

alternate rows of dark and light beads, dark and light stripes will alternate down the rope. (There will be two dark rows next to each other, with beads #1 and #17 at the tops.)

TUBULAR PEYOTE, EVEN COUNT

The advantage of even-count is that it allows for a flat bottom on the pouch. It differs from odd-count peyote in one simple particular.

1 Thread a stiff beading needle with about 1 yard (.9 m) of thread. Don't knot it.

2 Alternating dark and light, string 30 large seed beads. Tie the beads in a circle, using an overhand knot. See Figure 7.

3 Make a cardboard core and adjust it to fit the beads (see page 65).

4 Moving right to left, take the needle through the first bead to the left of the knot—bead #1. Pick up a light bead and take the needle through bead #3. Pick up another light bead and take the needle through bead #5. See Figure 8. Continue around the circle until you're back to bead #1.

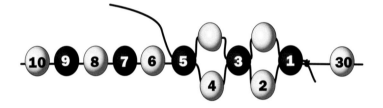

F I G U R E   8

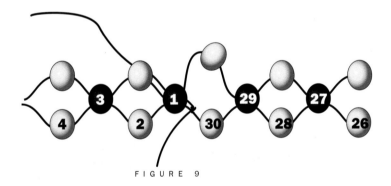

F I G U R E   9

5 Pick up a light bead and take the needle again through bead #1. Then take the needle through the next high bead—a light bead. See Figure 9. That last maneuver was a step-up; it finished the row and brought the thread up one level, ready to start the next row. You'll need to repeat this step-up at the end of every row.

6 Pick up a dark bead and take the needle through the next high bead (a light one). Continue beading tubular peyote until you're comfortable with the technique. As the beaded tube builds up on the cardboard support, slide the rows down toward the bottom.

TWO-DROP TUBULAR PEYOTE

Follow the directions for tubular peyote, but substitute two beads for one at every step. For example, to make your base strand, string on two dark beads, two light, two dark, and so on. To begin weaving, take the needle through the first two dark beads to the left of the knot. Pick up two light beads, skip over the next two beads, and take the needle through the next two. See Figure 10.

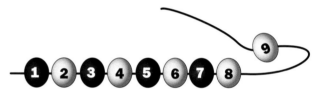

FIGURE 10

Flat Peyote Stitch

Unlike tubular peyote, flat peyote is worked, er, flat: back and forth, rather than around a solid support.

FLAT PEYOTE STITCH, EVEN COUNT

1 Thread a short, stiff beading needle with beading thread.

2 String on a dark bead, then take the needle through the bead again in the same direction, to secure it. Leave a 4-inch (10.5 cm) tail.

3 String seven more beads, alternating light and dark (see Figure 11) for a total of eight. This is your base strand.

FIGURE 11

WEAVING FLAT
PEYOTE WITH
DELICA BEADS

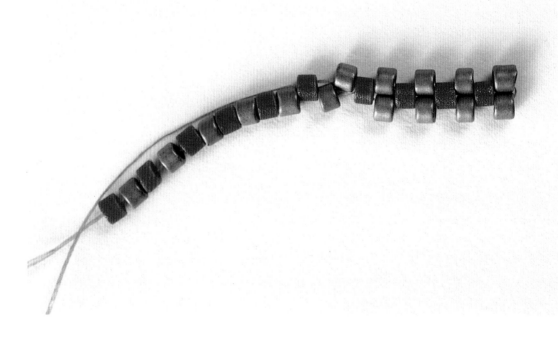

TOP:
EVEN-COUNT
FLAT PEYOTE.
BOTTOM:
TWO-DROP
PEYOTE

4 Some people find it handy to tape the tail to the work surface with masking tape, with the tail heading northwest. Others don't.

5 Working from right to left, pick up a light bead (#9) and take the needle back through bead #7 (the next dark bead). Pick up another light bead and

take the needle through #5. Continue to pick up a light bead and take the needle back through the next dark bead until you have completed the row. See Figure 12.

6 To bead the next row, turn the work around so you can work from right to left again. Pick up a dark

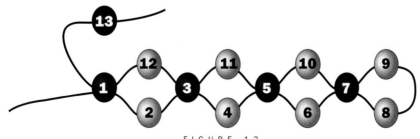

FIGURE 12

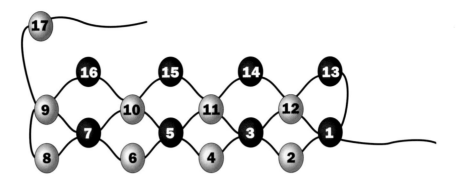

FIGURE 13

bead (#13) and take the needle through #12 (the next light bead). Continue adding dark beads until the row is complete. See Figure 13.

7 Continue to add rows until you're familiar with the stitch.

DECREASING THE ROWS, EVEN COUNT

Unless you're weaving a square or rectangle, eventually you'll need to make some rows shorter than others. With even count, it's easy.

After you exit the last bead in the row, take the needle under the edge thread and pull it through. Loop the thread around the edge thread, then take it back through beads A and B. You're now ready to add a new bead for the new, shorter row. See Figure 14.

FLAT PEYOTE STITCH, ODD COUNT

Odd count isn't hard, but it's a small nuisance at the end of every other row. In the absence of a good reason not to, make your base strand an even number of beads and work in even count.

1 Thread a short, stiff beading needle with beading thread.

2 String on a light bead, then take the needle through the bead again in the same direction, to secure it. Leave a 4-inch (10.5 cm) tail.

3 String eight more beads, alternating light and dark (see Figure 15) for a total of nine. This is your base strand.

4 Pick up a light bead (#10). Skip over the next bead and take the needle through bead #8. See Figure 16. Continue to needle through every other bead until you come to the end of the row.

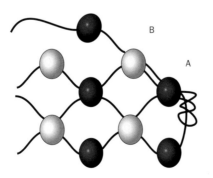

FIGURE 14

FIGURE 15

5 Horrors! Because the thread exits bead #2 rather than bead #1 there is no high bead to attach the next row to. Your only choice is to attach it to other beads in the neighborhood—the ones in the previous row. This requires a few extra flicks of the thread.

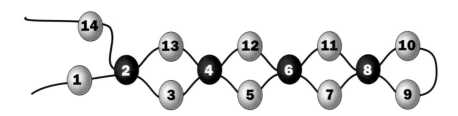

FIGURE 16

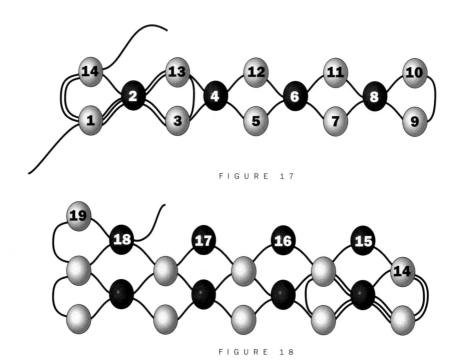

FIGURE 17

FIGURE 18

6 Take the needle down through bead #1, from left to right. Needle through bead #2, then #3. Now head back the other way: through #13, #2, #1 (again!) then back through #14. Good old #14 is now anchored and you can proceed to weave. See Figure 17.

7 At the end of the next row (and all even-numbered rows), there will be a high bead and you can do a normal turn, as for even-count peyote. See Figure 18.

8 At the end of subsequent odd-numbered rows, pick up the last bead of the row and do a half-hitch around the edge thread of the two rows below you. See Figure 19.

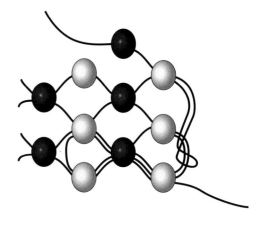

FIGURE 19

FIGURE 20

TWO-DROP PEYOTE

This is done exactly like regular even-count peyote, but it's done two beads at a time—which means the beading goes twice as fast.

1 To make a sample, string on 20 beads, alternating two dark and two light.

2 Pick up two light beads and take the needle back through beads #18 and #17. Pick up two more light beads and take the needle back through beads #14 and #13. See Figure 20. Proceed as with normal flat peyote.

PEYOTE TIPS

Always take the needle through the high bead.

When you pull the thread to snap the bead into place, pull it in the direction that you're weaving—that is, in the direction it's already going. If you pull it backward, you'll tend to open the weaving you've already done.

Make up a mantra. You'll be beading along on your sampler, awash in self-confidence, when you'll suddenly lose it—you'll have no idea where you are or what you're supposed to do next. The mantra for those moments: "Pick one up, needle through the high. Pick one up, needle through the high."

Don't get the tail caught in the weaving. Tape it out of the way, if necessary.

Turn the work around each time you finish a row so that you always weave in one direction—right to left. It helps to keep your place and keep track of what you're doing.

READ ON

Numerous booklets explain peyote stitch, all in essentially the same terms. Perhaps the clearest and most enjoyable treatment is Nicolette Stessin's *Beaded Amulet Purses* (Seattle, WA: Beadworld Publishing, 1994). If you like peyote purses, this fine little book is a "must have."

QUILLED BARRETTE

BEFORE THERE WERE GLASS BEADS, THERE WERE PORCUPINE QUILLS, AND NATIVE AMERICANS APPLIED THEM IN HANDSOME, SOMETIMES ELABORATE PATTERNS. THIS BARRETTE COMBINES BEADS AND QUILLS—BOTH AVAILABLE AT BEAD STORES.

DESIGN:

Kimberly Shuck

HOW-TO:

Backstitch, page 64;
barrette backs,
page 16.

YOU WILL NEED

2 pieces automotive
chamois cloth, each
about 4 by 5 inches
(10.5 x 13 cm)

Strong scissors

Piece of rawhide about
the size of the barrette

Seed beads, size 11

Porcupine quills

Chalk or pencil

Bead cement

Barrette back

Beading thread

Beading needle

Leather glue

Leather punch or awl

Heavy scissors

Piece of rawhide about
3-1/8 by 3-1/2 inches
(8 x 9 cm)

1 Automotive chamois sometimes smells of linseed oil. If yours does, set it in the sun until the odor dissipates.

2 Cut out two oval pieces of chamois the size you want the barrette to be. The one shown is 3-1/4 inches wide and 2-7/8 inches high (8.5 x 7.25 cm).

3 Starting at the outer edge of the cloth, back-stitch five rows of beads around one of the chamois pieces.

4 Select about 17 quills of similar thickness in graduated lengths, so that you can lay them out in a fan pattern. After arranging them on the chamois, put a small dot of chalk or pencil at each end of each quill, so you'll know where each belongs.

5 Sew the quills to the chamois, starting at one end. Knot the thread and position the end quill on the barrette. Working from back to front, bring the needle through the chamois right next to the quill end. Take the needle through the hollow quill and back down through the chamois at the other end.

6 Position the second quill. Bring the needle back up through the chamois right next to its end (the one closest to your needle's current position). See Figure 1. Work as close to the quills as you can, so the stitches are virtually invisible. Continue in this manner until all the quills are stitched to the chamois. Knot the thread on the back of the barrette and dot the knot with bead cement.

7 Cut the rawhide into an oval 1/4 inch (1 cm) smaller than the chamois; the chamois should project about 1/8 inch (.5 cm) all the way around.

8 Glue the rawhide to the back of the beaded chamois and allow to dry.

9 Glue the barrette back to the rawhide and allow to dry.

10 Cut two slits in the remaining piece of chamois, one for each raised end of the barrette back to project through. Open the barrette and slip the chamois over the barrette back. With a running stitch, stitch around the edge of the barrette, sewing the back chamois to the front.

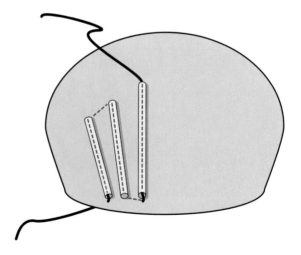

FIGURE 1

CABOCHON BROOCH

THE STONES IN THIS BROOCH ARE AZURITE AND LAPIS, BUT ANY ARRESTING CABOCHONS WOULD DO. IN DESIGNING THE OVERALL SHAPE OF THE BROOCH, BE GUIDED BY THE SHAPES OF YOUR CABOCHONS.

DESIGN:

Cheri Lynn Waltz

HOW-TO:

Backstitch, page 64; making fringe, page 22; attaching fringe, page 63; using pin backs, page 16

YOU WILL NEED

Leather scraps

Cabochons

Beading thread

Beading needles

Seed beads and bugle beads

4 to 8mm semi-precious beads

Jeweler's adhesive

Clear rigid plastic (such as the lid from greeting card or note-card box, or the lid of a yogurt carton)

Small, sharp scissors

Pin back

1 On a piece of paper, arrange the stones in various ways until you're pleased with the layout. Draw around them to outline the shape of the brooch.

2 Cut out the paper pattern and lay it on the right side of a piece of leather that's slightly larger than your brooch. Trace around the pattern. Position the cabochons as you want them, leaving room for at least one row of seed beads between them. Trace around the cabochons.

3 Glue the principal cabochon in position on the leather. Allow to dry.

4 Backstitch four rows of seed beads around the cabochon.

5 Sew a row of bugle beads around the backstitched seed beads.

6. Glue the second cabochon to the leather and backstitch around it.

7 Glue the third cabochon in place. Cover the remaining brooch with backstitched beads, using the photo as a guide.

8 If desired, add fringe, attaching it to the bottom row of beading.

9 Trim the excess leather close to the beadwork, being careful not to cut the thread.

10 Cut a piece of plastic to fit the brooch and glue it to the back. Cut a second piece of leather and mark where the pin back will go. Punch or cut holes for the pin back and press the leather over the pin, with the right side of the leather to the outside. Glue the leather to the back of the brooch.

SERPENT PIN

A GREAT SNAKE SEEMS TO MOVE. FOR MAXIMUM SLITHER, USE TINY (SIZE 16 OR 20) BEADS. FOR FASTER COVERAGE, SUBSTITUTE LARGER ONES.

1 Sketch your personal serpent on a piece of paper until he/she looks right. Then outline it on the ultrasuede.

2 Backstitch around the outline of the snake. String more beads at one time for long straight lines, fewer (and perhaps smaller) beads for tight curves.

3 Once the snake is outlined, fill it in completely with parallel lines of beads. Finish with the head: red eyes and a coral "forked" tongue.

4 Trim the suede to within 1/8 inch (3 mm) of the

design all the way around, being careful not to cut the thread.

5 Lay the snake on another piece of ultrasuede and trace around it. Cut out the second piece of suede, as a backing. Cut two slits in the suede backing (for the projecting ends of the pin back). Open the pin and lay the suede over the pin back, forcing the ends through the slits.

6 Stitch the two pieces of suede together around the edge, using either a simple running stitch or a two-bead edging. As you close the two, stuff with a little fiberfill.

DESIGN:

Collis Marshall

HOW-TO:

Backstitch, page 64 using pin backs, page 16; two-bead edging, page 24.

YOU WILL NEED

Piece of ultrasuede or deerskin

Pencil

Seed beads, size 16 to 20

Beading needle, size 16

Beading thread

Fine, sharp scissors

Pin back

Cotton or polyester fiberfill

Cylindrical (delica) beads for the edging (optional)

SUNSET JASPER PENDANT

CABOCHONS—POLISHED SEMIPRECIOUS STONES THAT ARE FLAT ON ONE SIDE—
MAKE EXCELLENT PENDANTS AND BROOCHES, WITH JUST A LITTLE BEADING.

DESIGN:

Janeen Shagman

HOW-TO:

Backstitch, page 64;
tubular peyote stitch,
even count, page 67;
making a continuous
necklace, page 20;
making fringe, page 22;
attaching fringe,
page 63.

YOU WILL NEED

Cabochon

Jeweler's glue

Thin, good-quality
leather or suede

Beading thread

Beading needle

Seed beads, size 11

Accent beads

Sharp scissors

Leather glue or white
craft glue

1 Cut a piece of leather that's about 1 inch (2.5 cm) larger than the cabochon in all directions. Glue the cabochon to the wrong side of the leather, using the jeweler's glue. Allow to dry overnight.

2 Thread the needle and knot the thread.

3 Working from back to front, bring the needle up through the leather very close to the cabochon.

4 Pick up six seed beads and backstitch around the cabochon, fitting the beads snugly against the stone. Adjust the fit of the beads so that you end up with an even number of them. This backstitched row provides your base strand.

5 Bead up over the edge of the cabochon, using tubular peyote stitch. For a fairly flat cab, two rows are usually enough.

6 Trim the leather very close to the original row of beads, being careful not to cut the threads.

7 Weave the thread back to the beginning row.

8 Now bead outward from the original row, to provide a frame for the stone. Weave three or four rows of tubular peyote, again using the original row as the base.

9 For a simple finish, just end with a row of peyote; its characteristic sawtooth edge will be quite handsome.

10 If you want the "star" effect shown in the photo, it's not hard to achieve. For the last row of peyote, add three beads instead of one in every

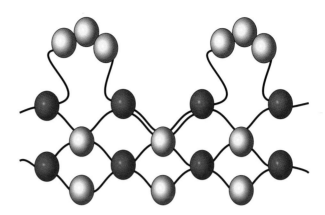

FIGURE 1

other space, poking them into a triangular shape. See Figure 1. Add no beads at all in alternate spaces, taking the thread back down through the previous row to avoid bare threads.

11 When you finish the last row, weave the thread through several beads, then down through the leather, and knot it.

12 Make a neck strap of seed beads and larger accent beads. Attach it to the pendant by weaving the thread through the beading (not the last row) and into the leather.

13 If desired, make fringe and attach it to the beads at the bottom of the pendant.

14 Glue a second piece of leather to the back of the pendant.

Tip
Some cabochons—rose quartz and amethyst, for example—are transparent enough to see through. When working with one of those, use either a white backing or one that matches the color of the cabochon. In either case, use suede or leather with very little grain.

AMETHYST CRYSTAL EARRINGS

CRYSTALS ARE POPULAR WITH JUST ABOUT EVERYONE. TO TURN THEM INTO EARRINGS, JUST ENCLOSE THEM IN TUBES OF PEYOTE.

DESIGN:

Jody Stewart-Keller

HOW-TO:

Odd-count tubular peyote, page 66

YOU WILL NEED

2 amethyst crystals, 10 to 12mm in diameter

Seed beads, size 14

Nylon beading thread

Beading needle, size 13 or 15

2 6mm Austrian lead crystal faceted beads

2 4mm round glass beads

Bead cement

Pair of French ear wires

Chain-nose pliers

1 String on enough beads to encircle the wide end of a crystal, using an odd number of beads. Tie the circle of beads around the crystal, leaving a 3-inch (7.5 cm) tail. While the circle should fit snugly, it doesn't have to be extremely tight, since you'll be gluing the peyote tube on later.

2 Working toward the tip of the crystal, weave a spiral of peyote until you've covered at least half the crystal.

3 Needle up through the rows until you exit the top row. Take the thread around the top row again, for added strength, and clip the initial tail.

4 String on six seed beads, then a 6mm lead crystal bead, then a 4mm round bead, then nine more seed beads. Take the thread back through the round bead, the crystal bead, and the first six seed beads. You've just created the first leg of the hanger.

5 Needle through Row 1 of the tube until you're about one-third of the way around, then exit. String on another six seed beads, then go again through the two accent beads, around the loop of nine beads, and back down the way you came to exit at the bottom of this second leg. See Figure 1.

6 Needle through the beads of Row 1 another one-third of the circumference and create the third leg.

7 After you've exited at the bottom of the third leg of six beads, anchor the thread in the peyote tube and clip the end.

8 Remove the amethyst crystal from the tube, dab a little bead cement around the crystal, and put the crystal back into the tube. Allow to dry.

9 Using the chain nose pliers, open the wire circle on the ear wire. Slip the nine-bead loop over the circle and close it.

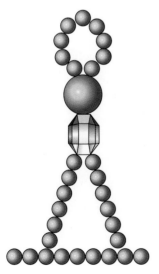

FIGURE 1

FLAT PEYOTE NECKPIECE

DESPITE THE POPULARITY OF PEYOTE POUCHES, A FLAT PEYOTE NECKPIECE ALLOWS FOR A PATTERN THAT HAS REMARKABLE CLARITY AND DETAIL. THIS PORTRAYAL OF TELVI, ANGEL OF SPRING, SUGGESTS JUST HOW SOPHISTICATED THE PATTERNS CAN BECOME. AREAS OF THREE-DIMENSIONAL WORK ADD EXTRA INTEREST.

DESIGN:

Carol Wilcox Wells

HOW-TO:

Flat peyote stitch, page 68; making fringe, page 22; attaching fringe, page 63

YOU WILL NEED

Beading thread

Beading needle

Cylinder seed beads, size 11

Tiny stars with loops

Bugle beads (for fringe)

Wire cutters

Head pin 4 inches (10.5 cm) long

Silver chain

2 jump rings

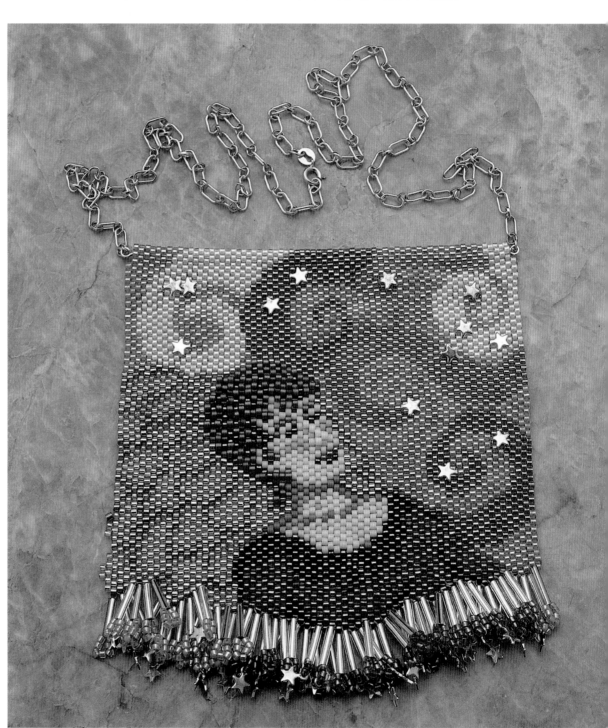

1 For a design of this complexity, it's a good idea to draw it out on graph paper, rather than to bead spontaneously. Peyote graph paper is widely available. With a set of colored pencils or pens, you can design at will.

2 The neckpiece shown in the photo has a base strand of 71 beads and thus must be woven with odd-count peyote stitch. If you want to avoid the extra turns involved in odd-count, simply string on 70 beads instead.

3 Using flat peyote, weave your design. The stars each have a small loop attached to one of their points. Bend each loop back at a right angle to the star. Add them to neckpiece as you weave by picking up a bead and a star at the same time.

4 After the piece is woven, go back and add additional beads for the nose, on top of the original weaving. Decide where you want the extra beads and bring the needle out an adjacent bead. String on a bead and take the needle through the next bead. See Figure 1. Continue to add beads where

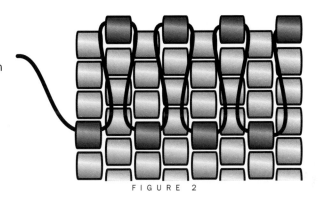

FIGURE 2

you want them, weaving in and out of the original piece as necessary.

5 Add fringe to the bottom. Each dangle has a bugle bead and either seven seeds or six seeds and a star.

6 With the wire cutters, snip off the head of the head pin. Form a loom in each end of the head pin and slip a jump ring into each loop. Attach the chain to the jump rings.

7 Fold the top of the piece back over the head pin. To do that, stitch the high beads in the top row to the fourth beads in alternate rows. See Figure 2. When you've stitched through several beads, pull the thread tight, rolling the weaving over the headpin. Continue the width of the piece.

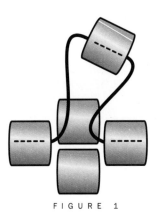

FIGURE 1

VENETIAN FOIL NECKLACE

THE ABUNDANT FRINGE ON THIS PENDANT ADDS GRACE AND MOVEMENT TO THE STUNNING GLASS CENTERPIECE.

DESIGN:

Jana Hunt Newton

HOW-TO:

Tubular peyote stitch, page 65; bead tips, page 15; making fringe, page 22; attaching fringe, page 63

YOU WILL NEED

Flat, rectangular piece of Venetian foil glass

Soft leather

Jeweler's glue

Beading thread

Beading needle

Seed beads, size 10

3 spear-shaped, faceted citrines

Faceted seed beads, size 12

Bead glue or clear fingernail polish

Accent beads, for the strap

1 Cut a piece of leather slightly larger than the Venetian foil glass, and glue the glass to the leather. Allow to dry.

2 Working from back to front, bring the needle up through the leather very close to the foil glass.

3 Pick up three seed beads and backstitch around the glass, fitting the beads snugly against it. Adjust the fit of the beads so that you end up with an even number. This backstitched row provides your base strand.

4 Trim the leather very close to the original row of beads, being careful not to cut the threads.

5 Bead up the sides of the glass all the way to the top, using tubular peyote stitch.

6 Attach the three spear-shaped citrines to the pendant, placing one at the top and one on each side. For each citrine, anchor the thread in the stitching around the centerpiece and weave about halfway up the citrine with tubular peyote. See Figure 1.

7 String on six large accent beads and lay them across the top of the centerpiece, anchoring the thread to the beadwork at each end. At each end of this strand and between the accent beads, secure the strand to the beadwork with loops of beads running front to back. If there are gaps in the beadwork, fill in with additional bits of peyote or even strung beads.

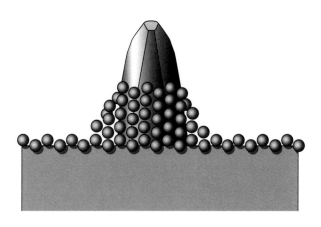

FIGURE 1

8 Make the fringe, stitching it to the bottom row of beading. Place the smaller seed and bugle beads close to the glass, then add the larger beads.

9 To make the strap, first attach a loop of seed beads to the beading on each side of the Venetian glass, adding an amber disk to the end of each loop. Then cut two pieces of #10 test monofilament (fishing line) 2 feet (61.5 cm) long. While monofilament can break, it is wonderfully invisible for clear, translucent beads. String seed beads onto each strand, pushing them to the center of the monofilament. Take both strands through the amber disk, then take all four pieces of monofilament through a single bead. Then string the large citrine and glass beads on all four pieces of monofilament. Repeat for the other strap.

10 When the strap is as long as you want it, divide the four threads into two pairs and tie the pairs together. Finish with bead tips.

SIMPLE PEYOTE POUCH

ALSO CALLED SPIRIT BAGS AND AMULET BAGS, PEYOTE POUCHES ARE WILDLY POPULAR. THIS IS THE EASIEST KIND TO MAKE: A PEYOTE TUBE WITH FRINGE AND A STRAP. THE BOTTOM IS OPEN (THE BETTER FOR YOUR GOOD FORTUNE TO ENTER AT WILL).

DESIGN:

Jody Stewart-Keller

HOW-TO:

Odd-count tubular peyote, page 66; making fringe, page 22; attaching fringe, page 63; even-count flat peyote, page 68.

YOU WILL NEED

Seed beads, size 11

Beading thread

Beading needle

A jar or a cardboard tube from a roll of toilet tissue or paper towels

2 4mm faceted beads

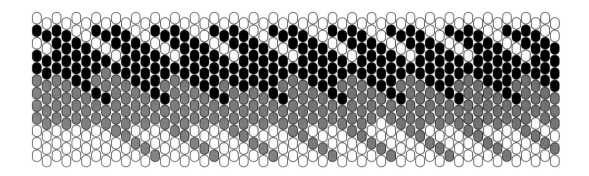

1 Thread a stiff beading needle with about 1 yard (.9m) of thread. Do not knot it.

2 String on 55 beads. This is the base strand that will encircle the entire pouch. Tie the beads into a circle, using a double knot.

3 If you're using a cardboard tube, prepare it as directed on page 65. Slip the circle of beads over it.

4 Using odd-count peyote, weave the bag as tall as you want it. After the base strand, each spiral row will have 27 beads. In the design shown, there are nine "points" of each color around the bag.

5 Make the fringe, attaching the strands to the "high beads" on the bottom row.

6 Using even-count flat peyote, weave a strap that's four rows wide.

7 To attach the strap, select two points on the cylindrical pouch to be the sides. (Make sure there will be an equal number of beads on the front and back of the pouch.) Now make a double loop of beads. To do that, first string on four seed beads, a

4mm bead, and three more seed beads. Take the needle through two beads on the base strand. String on three seed beads, take the needle back through the 4mm bead, and string on four more seeds. See Figure 1. Needle through the bottom row on the strap. For extra security, go around the loop again. Bury the thread in the bag.

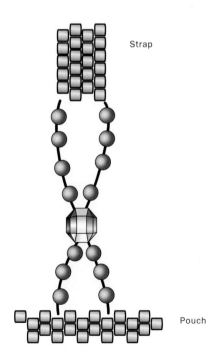

Strap

Pouch

FIGURE 1

PEYOTE POUCH WITH LID

WITH A FLAT BOTTOM AND A LID THAT SLIDES UP AND DOWN THE STRAP, THIS PEYOTE POUCH CAN CARRY SMALL OBJECTS: A CRYSTAL, A CHARM, EVEN A LIPSTICK. CALLED "PYRAMIDS OF FIRE" BY DESIGNER CAROL WILCOX WELLS, IT IS ABOUT 2-1/4 INCHES (6 CM) WIDE AND 4 INCHES (10.5 CM) TALL.

DESIGN:

Carol Wilcox Wells

HOW-TO:

Tubular peyote stitch, even count, page 67; flat peyote stitch, even count, page 68; making fringe, page 22; attaching fringe, page 63

YOU WILL NEED

Bronze, cream, and red cylinder seed beads, size 11

Beading thread

Beading needle

Cardboard tube from a roll of toilet tissue or paper towels

Bronze bugles, Swarovski crystals, gold teardrop beads (for the dangles)

1 Thread a stiff beading needle with about 1 yard (.9 m) of thread. Do not knot it.

2 String on 80 beads. This is the base strand that will encircle the entire pouch. Both front and back will be 36 beads across. Each side will be four beads deep.

3 Tie the beads in a circle, using a double knot.

4 Prepare the cardboard tube (see page 65). Slip the circle of beads over it.

5 Weave the body of the bag as high as you want it, using even- count tubular peyote.

Making the Bottom of the Bag

The bottom consists of a flat tab 36 beads wide that extends down from the front. It is folded up and stitched to the back and sides.

6 Gently mash the round pouch flat, to get an idea of where you want the front, sides, and back. Select the 36-bead width that will form the front of the pouch. On one end of this row, the outermost bead will be a high bead—that is, it will jut out from the row. At the other end, the outermost bead will be a low bead. Start weaving at the low-bead end.

7 Using even-count flat peyote stitch, weave back and forth across the front of the pouch, making the tab. Make eight rows, *counting on the diagonal.*

8 Fold the flap up so that it meets the back of the pouch, leaving four vertical rows of beads for each side of the pouch. Fit the bottom and the back of the pouch together like teeth in a zipper and stitch

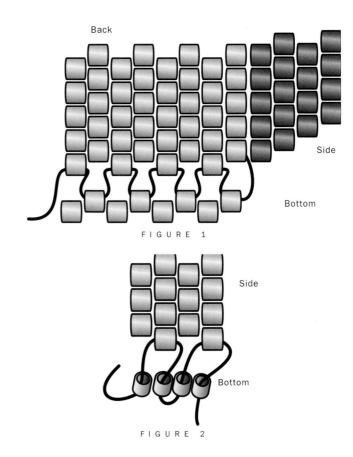

F I G U R E   1

F I G U R E   2

them closed, needling through the high beads of the pouch and the high beads of the bottom. See Figure 1.

9 Stitch the bottom to each side. Note that the beads of the sides and the beads of the bottom are inconveniently perpendicular to each other. Stitch them together as shown in Figure 2, closing the high beads first, then reversing direction and closing the low beads.

Adding the Fringe

10 Make the fringe, attaching it to the flat bottom.

Making the Strap

11 Using even-count flat peyote, weave a strap that's four vertical rows wide and as long as you like. If you plan to omit the lid, fit the ends of the strap to the sides of the pouch as you would the edges of a zipper, and stitch them together.

BASKETWEAVE # 2
DESIGN: CAROL WILCOX WELLS

Making the Lid

The lid is a miniature version of what you've already done: a piece of tubular peyote with a flat flap that's stitched to the back.

12 String on 90 beads to form the base strand. Decide how tall you want the top to be and weave a piece of tubular peyote that tall.

13 Using even-count flat peyote, weave a rectangular flap 36 beads wide and 10 beads deep (counting on the diagonal) that extends from the front of the lid. Fold it over and sew it to the back, as you did the bottom. Do NOT stitch the flap to the sides.

14 Fit one side of the strap to one side of the pouch; the two edges should fit together like the teeth of a zipper. Weave the thread in and out of high beads in one direction, then weave back the same way, for extra security.

15 String the strap up through one side of the top and down through the other side. Then attach the strap to the other side.

An Easier Bottom

If you don't mind a less three-dimensional pouch, you can skip the flat peyote bottom and simply stitch the front and back together, taking the thread through the high beads of front and back.

VARIATIONS
BASKETWEAVE #2

This handsome cranberry-and-navy pouch is a variation of "Pyramids of Fire" on page 88. Like that pouch, it is woven in even-count tubular peyote with a flat-peyote bottom, but it is woven in two-drop peyote, which produces a quite distinctive pattern—most obvious on the fold-over top flap. (See pages 68 and 72 for instructions.)

A second variation is equally interesting. While the pouch is woven primarily with size 11 cylinder beads—most visible on the top flap—a much larger cranberry bead (a size 3.3 cylinder) is often substituted for two small beads. While the large bead substitutes for two small ones, it is allotted only

MY HOUSE AMONG OTHERS
DESIGN: NAN C MEINHARDT

one row (the same as its smaller colleagues). This produces rows that are slightly askew and that contrast nicely with the regimented flap.

The flap is a flat-peyote extension of the back, which simply folds over the front. The heavy silver accent beads hold it in place.

For this purse, the base row is 96 size 11 beads. Both front and back consist of 42 beads; each side consists of six beads. Since the stitch is two-drop peyote, there are half that many vertical rows. (Note the strap; it is six beads, but three rows, wide.)

MY HOUSE AMONG OTHERS

Note the houses—created with rectangles of different color—that Nan C Meinhardt wove into this bag, using two-drop peyote and sizes 11, 15, and 20 seed beads. Each window is a bugle bead substituted for two seed beads.

The base row is 100 beads: 45 beads across front and back, five beads for each side. The bottom is a nine-row flap of flat peyote.

A new wrinkle is the use of embroidery floss to embellish the pouch. Split embroidery floss into separate strands; thread one strand (or as many as will fit) onto the bead needle. Secure the thread from the inside of the bag and bring it to the front. Using a whip stitch, outline some of the buildings.

ROCOCO NECKLACE WITH LEAVES

INSTEAD OF THIS ELEGANT NECKLACE, YOU CAN MAKE AN EQUALLY STRIKING BRACELET. JUST MAKE THE PEYOTE TUBE SHORTER AND ADD FEWER LEAVES.

DESIGN:

Marcie Stone

HOW-TO:

Odd-count tubular pey-ote, page 66; flat pey-ote, page 70.

YOU WILL NEED

Braided polyester rope, 1/4 inch (1 cm) in diameter

Beading thread

Beading needles, size 12 or 13

Seed beads, sizes 11 and 14

Delica or antique beads

Glass and semi-precious beads, sizes 4 to 6mm

Bugle beads

Larger glass or semi-precious beads, as focal points

Sharp scissors

1 Cut a piece of rope 20 to 22 inches (51.5-56.5 cm) long, depending upon how large you want the necklace to be. For a bracelet, cut the cord about 10 inches, or 25.5 cm, long.

2 String 13 or 15 beads onto the needle and tie them around the rope, for your base strand. If necessary, adjust the base strand to a larger odd number.

3 Using odd-count peyote stitch, spiral down the length of the tube until you've covered it completely. Bury the tail in the weaving.

Leaves

4 The leaves are woven in flat peyote. To start one, string on a bead, then go through it again in the same direction. Add six more beads, for a total of seven.

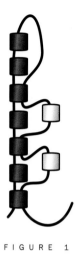

FIGURE 1

FIGURE 2

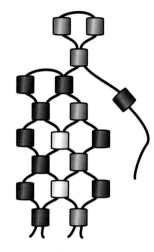

FIGURE 3

5 Skipping the last two beads that you strung, take the needle back through bead #5. Pick up a bead, skip a strung bead, and go back through bead #3. Pick up a bead and take the needle down through bead #1. See Figure 1. Pull the thread tight. See Figure 2.

6 Pick up a bead and go back up the row, taking the needle through the next high bead each time.

7 .When you come out the top bead of the row, add three beads and go back down through the first of the three beads you just added. The three beads will form a T shape at the top of the leaf. Now pick up a bead and continue down the row, going through the high bead each time. See Figure 3.

8 Continue to work up and down the rows, adding three beads each time you come to the tip. The leaf will grow longer and wider, acquiring a diagonal, downright leafy shape on one side.

9 When the leaf is as long as you want it, weave the other side into a diagonal as you did the first. As you work up toward the tip of the leaf, don't take the thread through the top-most bead—that is, stop

short of the T shape on the end. Add a bead and work your way back down the row. Continue to work up and down, decreasing in a symmetrical or asymmetrical manner.

ATTACHING THE LEAVES

10 As you continue to weave leaves of different sizes and shapes, position them around the tube in clusters until you're satisfied with the arrangement. If you like, arrange the leaves so that the ends of the necklace will be hidden under them.

11 Tack each leaf to the tube by weaving through several beads in the bottom of the leaf and several beads on the tube.

Embellishments

12 Stitch 4mm or 6mm beads, either singly or in loops, to the center of the leaves.

Finishing

13 At each end of the necklace, cut out some of the rope end, to make a shallow depression. Fold the tube flat and stitch the ends together. Add a clasp.

GEOMETRIC BARRETTE

DESIGNER JODY STEWART-KELLER USED SIZE 14 SEED BEADS FOR THIS GEOMETRICALLY PATTERNED BARRETTE, BUT THE LARGER SIZE 11S WOULD WORK AS WELL. KELLER CALLS THIS PIECE "AMAZON SOLSTICE."

DESIGN:

Jody Stewart-Keller

HOW-TO:

Flat peyote, even count, page 68; making fringe, page 22.

YOU WILL NEED

Seed beads, size 14

Beading thread

Beading needle

Graph paper for peyote weave

2 pieces of soft leather

1 piece of hard, pliable plastic (e.g., lid to yogurt carton)

Round-nose pliers

Leather needle

Razor knife

Citrine chips

Practice Project

1 The barrette is woven in even-count flat peyote. It is worked vertically, starting at the bottom point of the triangle, up to the top row, then back down again. As you work up and down, you'll weave out from the center, completing one-half of the triangle. Then you'll go back and weave the other half.

2 To "get it," start with a small example, using three colors of beads. String on a dark bead. To secure it, take the thread through it again in the same direction. This will be the bead at the bottom point of the triangle. Add nine more dark beads, to make a base row of 10.

3 Using even-count flat peyote, add a second row of five light beads.

4 When you reach the bottom and exit the first dark bead that you strung, do not pick up a bead, as you normally would. Instead, take the needle up through the last light bead. See Figure 1. Pick up a bead of the third color, and continue back up, with flat peyote.

5 To create the triangle, add a bead each time you reach the top of the triangle, in a normal peyote fashion. Do not add a bead when you reach the bottom; instead, take the needle back up through the last bead in the previous row; then proceed to add beads.

6 When you have woven half the triangle—see Figure 2—you will end up exiting the bead in the top corner. Bury the thread in the weaving.

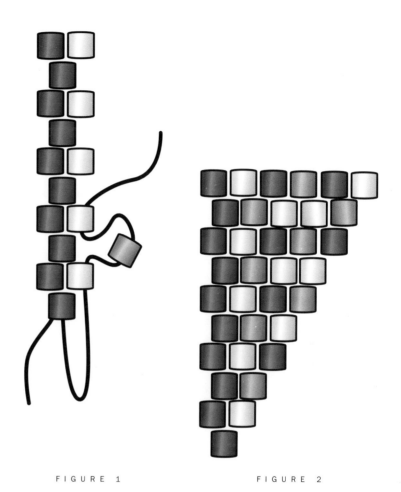

FIGURE 1   FIGURE 2

7 Working with a new thread, bury it at the bottom of the work, so that you come down out of the first bead. Needle up through the end bead on the next row, then add a bead. The bottom row should have one bead; the second row, two beads; the third row, three beads.

8 Complete the other half of the triangle as you did the first.

The Barrette

1 Draw your design on graph paper for peyote stitch. Make sure there are an even number of beads in the top horizontal row. If there are 56 beads in the top row, you'll end up with a barrette that's about 4 inches (10.5 cm) across. A top row of 42 beads will yield a barrette about 3 inches (7.5 cm) wide. Note the graph for this piece.

2 Weave the barrette as you did the practice project described above (but with a lot more beads).

3 Lay the beaded triangle on a piece of leather and trace around it; cut out the leather triangle. Cut a second leather triangle and a plastic triangle slightly smaller than the first. Against the beaded piece, place the small leather triangle, then the plastic, then the large leather triangle. Stitch the leather to the beading around the edges, taking the needle between every two beads around the perimeter.

4 Lay the barrette finding against the leather backing and mark where the raised section on each end

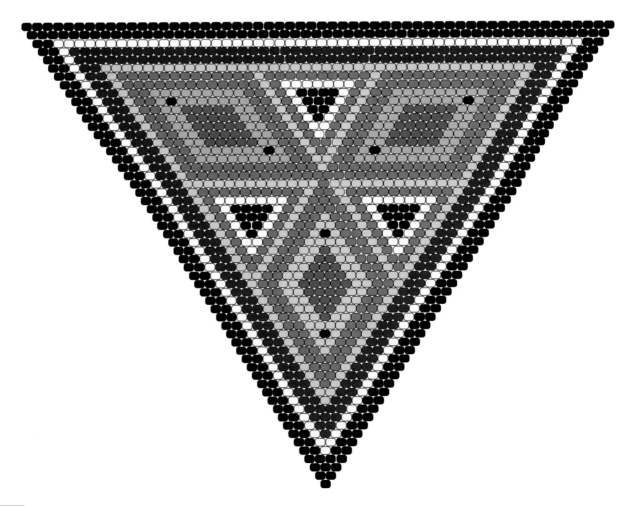

should protrude through the leather. Using the razor knife, cut two vertical slits in the leather, slightly wider then the finding. Open the barrette and, beginning with the extended arm, guide the barrette into one slit and out the other, gripping it with pliers if desired. Sew up the slits close to the barrette.

5 If desired, add fringe to the two lower sides, using the citrine chips at the bottom. (Be sure to attach the leather backing before making the fringe, or your thread will become hopelessly tangled.)

VARIATIONS

To make a neckpiece instead of a barrette, omit the barrette finding. Instead, weave a peyote strap of the desired length and width and attach it to the corners, using necklace findings.

COMANCHE WEAVE EARRINGS

ONCE YOU GET THE HANG OF COMANCHE WEAVE, YOU CAN MAKE EARRINGS TO MATCH A NEW OUTFIT FASTER THAN YOU CAN SHOP FOR THEM. THE STITCH IS ALSO KNOWN AS BRICK-LAYING STITCH (NOTE THE RESEMBLANCE TO A BRICK WALL). MOST COMANCHE EARRINGS CONSIST OF A WOVEN TRIANGLE WITH FRINGE AT THE BOTTOM.

FESTIVE GOLD EARRINGS

DESIGN:

Patti Hill

HOW-TO:

Making fringe, page 22; attaching fringe, page 63

YOU WILL NEED

Beading thread

Masking tape

Beading needle

Bugle beads (optional)

Seed beads, size 11

Bead cement

Earring findings

Making the Base Row

The base row is the widest woven row, usually the bottom of the triangle. As you go up the triangle, each row has one fewer bead than the row below it; the beads sit on the spaces between the beads in the row below. The base row can consist of a row of vertical bugle beads or a row of seed beads stacked two high.

1 To make a practice sample, thread the needle with 2 yards (1.8 m) of thread. (Don't double it.) If you plan to add fringe, leave a 2-foot (61.5 cm) tail. If not, a 6-inch (15.5 cm) tail will do.

2 With masking tape, tape the thread to the table, to hold it taut and to keep the beads from falling off.

3 String on seven bugle beads.

4 Skipping over the last bead you threaded (bead #7), bring the needle back through bead #6 in the same direction you went the first time. See Figure 1. Pull the thread taut. The last two bugle beads—which up to now have been lying end to end, like all the others—will now be bound snugly to each other side by side.

5 Repeat this process for the rest of the base row, looping each bugle bead to the previous one. See Figure 2. Pull the thread taut but not so tight that you cause the row to pucker. When you're finished, you should have a row of vertical bugle beads. See Figure 3.

The base row may need some encouragement to lie flat. Fear not. Just keep gently mashing it flat and eventually it will get the idea.

6 If you don't want to use bugle beads for the base row, use a row of seed beads stacked on top of each other. The technique is the same; just substitute two seed beads for each bugle bead. When you've threaded on all the seed beads of the base row, skip over the last pair of seed beads and bring the thread back through the next pair of seed beads. The beads will line up vertically two by two. See Figure 4.

Additional Rows

7 Thread a bead onto the needle. Bring the needle from back to front under the thread between the tops of the two end beads in the row below. Pull the thread through until the bead is more or less over the space between the two beads below it. Be sure the thread is going down through the new bead.

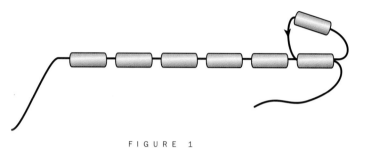

FIGURE 1

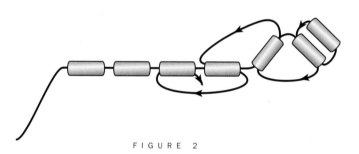

FIGURE 2

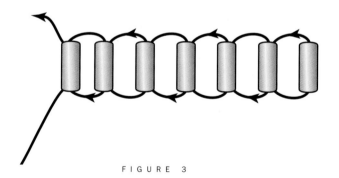

FIGURE 3

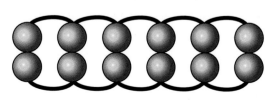

FIGURE 4

MARDI GRAS EARRINGS

DESIGN:

*Mary Young Smith
and Patti Hill*

Thread the needle back up through the same bead and pull it snug. See Figure 5.

At the beginning of each row, the thread should come up from the row below, over the top of the first bead, and down through the loop of thread below.

Continue to add beads in the same fashion until the row is complete. See Figure 6. Each row will have one fewer bead than the row below. See Figure 7.

8 Add new rows, weaving back and forth across the ornament, until you have a row of two beads, which completes the triangle. See Figure 7.

Making the Top Loop

9 When you finish the top row, the thread will be at one end of the row. Thread the beads for the

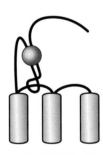

FIGURE 5

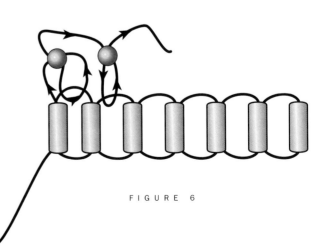

FIGURE 6

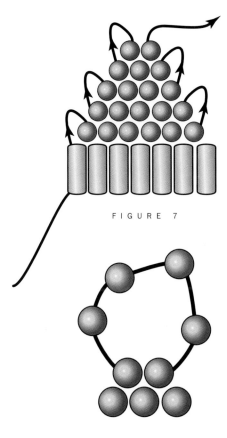

FIGURE 7

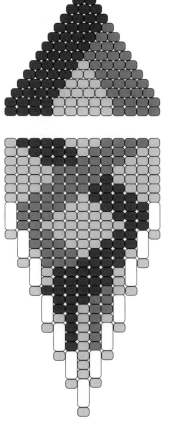

FIGURE 8

loop onto the needle, one after the other; the more beads, the bigger the loop.

10 Bring the needle back down through the bead at the opposite end of the top row, then up and

down through the beads of the top row until you're back at the first end of the row. See Figure 8.

11 Take the needle back through all the beads in the loop, for strength.

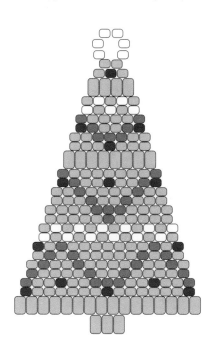

IRIS
EARRINGS

DESIGN:

Mary Young Smith

12 Again, weave through the top row and, this time, down into the next row as well. Weave over and under a few beads, apply a dot of bead glue, and clip the threads.

Adding Fringe

13 Thread a needle onto the initial tail on the base row and make the fringe, weaving it in and out of the base row.

Using Charts

Designing is often easier on paper. Use graph paper for Comanche weave (or peyote weave) for the woven section and plain paper for the fringe. For easier visualization of a future project, fill in the squares with colored pencils or pens.

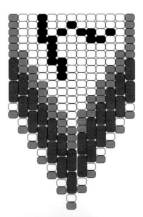

FESTIVE GOLD EARRINGS

The base row consists of 14 gold bugles. The second row consists of silver seed beads woven two at a time, as if they were a base row. A single row of gold seeds is followed by rows of gold interspersed with red, blue, and green.

MARDI GRAS EARRINGS

The base row consists of 13 pairs of seed beads; the two beads in each pair are stacked on top of each other. (To find the base row in the photo, look for the only row in which two beads are straight up and down.)

CHRISTMAS TREE EARRINGS

Start with a base row of 16 gold bugles, leaving a 1-foot (31 cm) tail. Weave the triangle and the loop. Thread a needle onto the initial tail and weave it toward the center of the tree. Add a trunk of three gold bugles, weaving in and out of the bugles.

IRIS EARRINGS

Images can be woven into Comanche weave quite handily. These irises can be created in the color of your choice.

DIAMOND EARRINGS

To create a diamond shape, weave two triangles. The base row is located at the center of the diamond; it has nine pairs of beads stacked directly on top of each other.

Starting with the base row, first make the upper triangle and the loop. (Leave yourself a long initial tail.) Then turn the work upside down and work the lower triangle, ending with a row of five beads. Then work the fringe in the usual fashion.

LOOMWORK BASICS

MANUFACTURERS OF INEXPENSIVE BEAD LOOMS COMMONLY LABEL THEIR PRODUCTS "FOR AGES 7 AND UP." THAT'S HOW EASY THE ACTUAL WEAVING IS (AND HOW FAST IT GOES). ON THE OTHER HAND, YOU'LL BE GRATEFUL FOR ADULTHOOD WHEN IT COMES TO CREATING THE DESIGN AND FINISHING OFF THE JEWELRY.

> SOME OF MY BEST AND MOST CREATIVE WORK HAPPENS WHEN I'VE MADE A MISTAKE AND I HAVE TO FIGURE OUT HOW TO WORK AROUND IT. I'VE STOPPED BEING AFRAID OF MAKING A MISTAKE.
>
> **NANCY MCGAHA**

Looming is done with two sets of threads. The warp threads are fixed to the loom for the duration of the work. The perpendicular weft thread is used for weaving; it holds the beads and wraps around the warps.

THE LOOM

Most sizable craft stores sell inexpensive bead looms. (So do many toy stores; if anyone asks, say it's for your nephew.) While a small loom limits you to small jewelry, it's an easy place to start. Once you decide to like loomwork, you'll probably want to make your own loom to accommodate larger pieces.

THREAD

Ordinary nylon beading thread works fine. When you get to serious projects, you may want to use a heavier weight for the warp than for the flexible weft.

AN INEXPENSIVE CRAFT LOOM

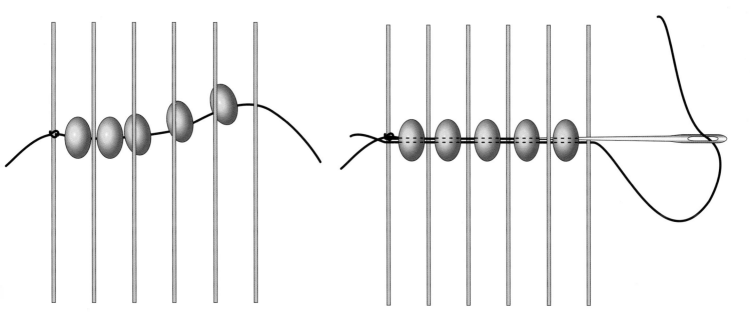

F I G U R E 1

F I G U R E 2

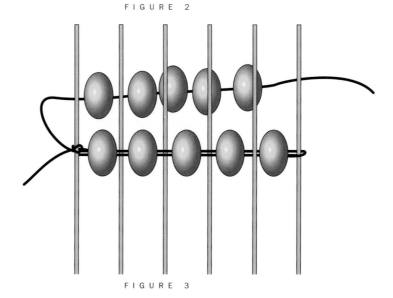

F I G U R E 3

WARPING

To string the warp onto a purchased loom, follow the manufacturer's instructions. For an example, see the sidebar on page 107.

The beads will occupy the spaces between the warps, which means you'll need one more warp thread than the number of beads in each horizontal row. (For example, if your design is 10 beads wide, you'll need 11 warp threads.)

WEAVING

Cut a piece of thread about 4 feet (1.23 m) long. With a single knot, tie it onto the left outside warp at the bottom of the design, leaving a tail about 5 inches (13 cm) long. This is the weft thread. (If you're left-handed, tie onto the right outside warp and reverse the following directions.)

Thread the needle onto the weft and string on all the beads in the bottom row of your design. Keep in mind that you're stringing them left to right across the design.

Push the beads down to the end of the thread. Bring the needle under all the warps and pull the line of beads up against the bottom of the warps. With your left hand, press the beads up between the warps, one bead for each space. See Figure 1.

Take the needle back through the line of beads, making sure that you pass over each warp. See Figure 2.

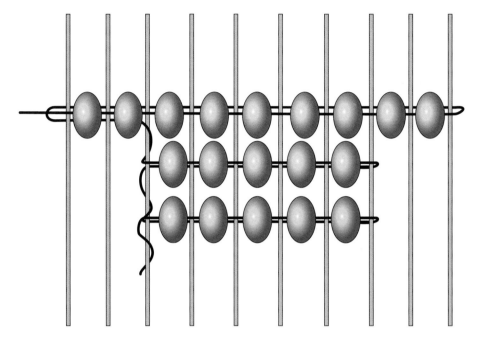

FIGURE 4

Now string on your second row of beads and attach them above the first in a similar fashion. See Figure 3. Continue until you have completed your design.

DECREASING THE WIDTH OF ROWS

This is child's play. Simply stop your row as many warps short as you want and weave as usual.

INCREASING THE WIDTH OF ROWS

This isn't as easy. Let's say you've woven several five-bead rows and now you want to weave some nine-bead rows. After exiting the last five-bead row (on the left), loop the thread around the warp to the left of that last bead. Now, working from *right to left*, string on the two extra beads required for the left side of the next row. Bring the line of beads under the warps and push them up into the spaces between. Take the needle around the far left warp and back through the extra beads you just added.

Now string on the remaining seven beads for the rest of this row and continue as usual. See Figure 4.

ADDING A NEW THREAD

The best time to notice that the weft is becoming inconveniently short is when you finish a row—that is, when you're back at the far left warp. Tie the weft around the warp in a single knot, leaving a 5-inch (13 cm) tail. You'll be back. Tie a new thread on the outer left warp and begin the next row, as you did at the beginning.

TYING OFF THE WEFT THREADS

When you finish weaving, cut the piece from the loom by cutting the warp threads close to the end of the loom. Unfortunately, you'll have warp ends at top and bottom (see below). You also left a weft tail each time you ended an old weft and started a new thread. If you can, undo the knots that tied the wefts to the warp. (If they won't budge, forget

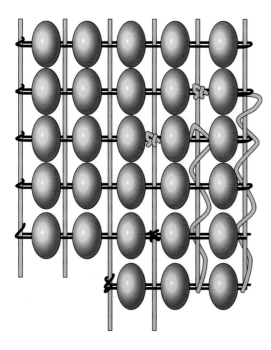

FIGURE 5

them.) Thread a needle onto the tail and take the thread back into the nearest row of beads. Come up between two beads and tie the tail around the intersection of warp and weft. Before pulling the knot tight, needle through an adjacent bead and dot the knot with bead cement. Then, when you pull gently, the knot should disappear into the bead hole. Clip the thread as closely as possible.

BURYING THE WARP THREADS

This is the tedious part of looming, and beaders have developed various ways to avoid it altogether. (See individual project instructions.) However, if you want a level top or bottom with no fringe, here's what to do.

Thread a needle onto a warp. Take the needle around the lowest weft and back up alongside itself, looping it around the warp as you go. Needle through an adjacent bead and tie a knot around a junction of warp and weft. See Figure 5.

WARPING A TYPICAL CRAFT LOOM

1 Cut five pieces of thread 40 inches (102.5 cm) long.

2 Fold the threads in half. Loop the folded centers around the screw on the wooden beam. (See the photo.) Tie the bundle of threads in an overhand knot, to hold them on the beam.

3 Bring the threads over the nearest spring. Lay each thread in a separate coil, placing them in adjacent coils. Once the threads are in adjacent coils, cover them with a piece of masking tape, to hold them in place temporarily.

4 Holding the threads taut, turn the beam a couple of times, to secure the warps.

5 Bring the threads across the top of the loom and through the coils of the second spring, lining them up with the first. Again, tape them in place.

6 Divide the warps into two groups and tie them onto the screw at the other end of the loom. Turn the second beam the warps are taut. Remove both pieces of tape.

7 The advantage of this loom is that, as you work, you scroll the beading onto one of the beams, which allows you to complete a much longer piece than the size of the loom would suggest.

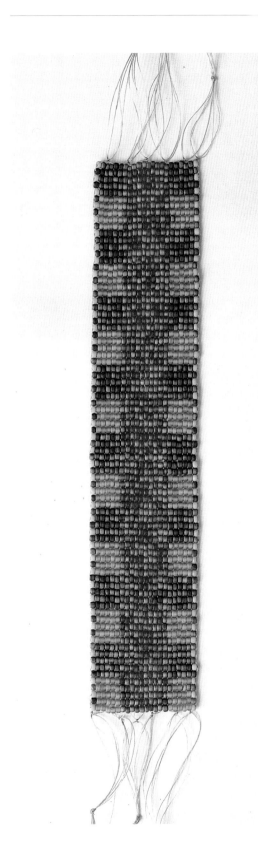

WARP THREADS
CAN BE BURIED
OR FRINGED.

DESIGN:
NANCY McGAHA

ENDING WARPS WITH FRINGE

This is a time-honored technique. Thread a needle onto a warp thread and string the beads for the fringe. Take the thread back up along the warp for several rows and knot it over a weft. Needle through several beads and knot again. See Figure 6.

READ ON

Probably more people have learned to loom from Virginia Blakelock than from anyone else. Her self-published, soft-cover classic— *Those Bad, Bad Beads!*—is available in bead stores everywhere. Its clear instructions and good humor are equally reliable.

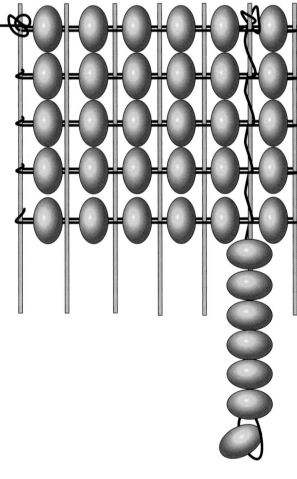

FIGURE 6

MAKING YOUR OWN

You can do this. (If not, your nephew can do this.) Nail four boards together in a rectangle. Make it long and wide enough to accommodate your jewelry and high enough so you can get your hands under the warp. Nail a spring along the top edge of each end to hold the warps, and add one or two protruding nails at each end to tie the warp ends to.

If springs are unavailable (or undesirable), attach cup hooks or nails to the top ends and use each one for several turns of the warp. The first row of beads will space out the warps, separate and equal.

To warp this kind of loom, work back and forth in a continuous loop. Working with an entire spool of thread, tie the end onto an end nail. Take the thread through a coil of the nearest spring, then through a corresponding coil of the far spring, around the other end nail, back up through an adjacent coil of the far spring, back to the near spring, and so on until you have the required number of warps.

LOOMED BRACELETS

A FLAT BAND OF BEADS WITH A HOOK-AND-LOOP CLOSURE—WHAT COULD BE SIMPLER TO MAKE? YET THE DESIGN POSSIBILITIES ARE ENDLESS.

DESIGN:

Nancy McGaha

HOW-TO:

Loomwork basics,
page 104.

YOU WILL NEED

Beading thread

Bead loom

Beading needle

Seed beads, size 11

3/4-inch-wide (2 cm)
hook and loop tape

Glue

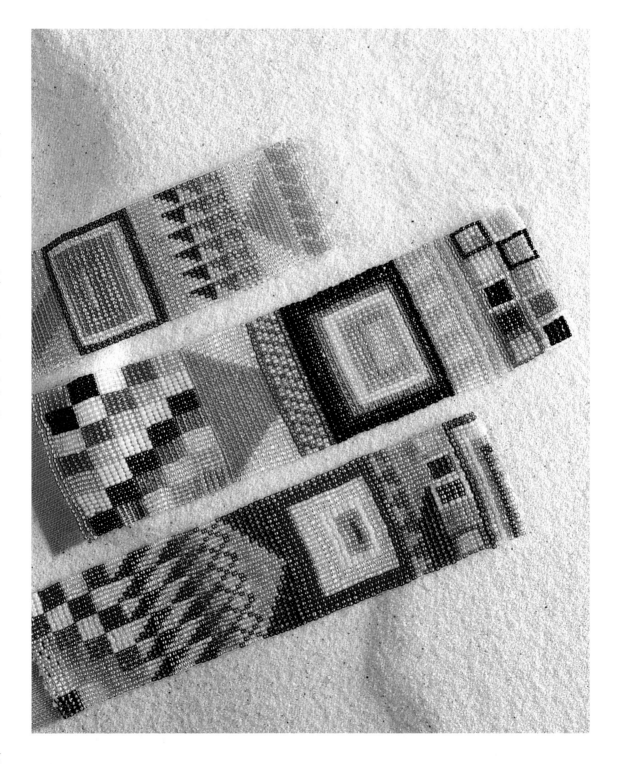

1 String 31 warps on a bead loom.

2 Cut a piece of thread about 1 yard (.9 m) long and tie it to the outer left warp, about 4 inches (10.5 cm) from the bottom of the loom.

3 Working left to right and bottom to top, complete one of the patterns shown, or create your own.

4 When the pattern is complete, cut the warp threads close to the loom ends, leaving 4-inch strands on the bracelet. Tie the warps together by twos or fours.

5 Cut a piece of hook-and-loop tape slightly shorter than the bracelet is wide, and separate the two layers. Fold the warps to the back of the bracelet and glue one layer of the tape to each end, making sure to position the tape so that when the bracelet is looped around a wrist, the layers of tape will cling to each other.

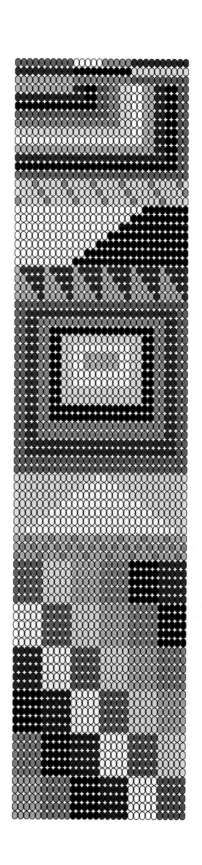

FLAT LOOMED NECKLACE

THIS IS PROBABLY THE EASIEST LOOMED NECKLACE TO MAKE: A FLAT PIECE OF WEAVING WITH THE WARP ENDS SIMPLY TUCKED BEHIND IT, THEN GLUED TO A PIECE OF LEATHER.

DESIGN:

Nancy McGaha

HOW-TO:

Loomwork basics, page 104; making fringe, page 22; attaching fringe, page 63.

YOU WILL NEED

Bead loom

Beading thread

Beading needle

Seed beads, size 11

Leather

Glue

1 String 41 warps on a bead loom.

2 Cut a piece of thread about 1 yard (.9 m) long and tie it to the outer left warp, about 4 inches (10.5 cm) from the bottom of the loom.

3 Weave the pattern as shown. Note that this piece is woven from side to side—that is, what will end up as the two sides of the necklace are in fact the top and bottom of the loomwork.

4 Remove the weaving from the loom and tie the warp ends in square knots by twos or fours.

5 Loom a strap seven beads wide and as long as you want it. Weave it in three sections, attaching them to each other by tying pairs of warps together. Finish the warp ends with fringe, burying the tails in the woven strap.

6 Stitch the straps to the body of the necklace. For each row, take the needle through a few beads on the strap and through a few beads on the body, up to the next row, then double back to the strap, connecting the two pieces in a zigzag pattern.

7 Add fringe to the bottom of the piece, anchoring it in the weaving.

8 Lay the woven necklace on a piece of leather and trace around it, covering the woven rectangle out to and including the straps. Cut out the leather. Fold the warp ends toward the center (trim them if necessary) and glue the leather to the back of the necklace.

DRAGONFLY MEDICINE BAG

AMULET POUCHES DON'T HAVE TO BE WOVEN WITH PEYOTE STITCH. THIS LONG, LOOMED PIECE IS FOLDED IN HALF AND STITCHED TOGETHER.

DESIGN:

Janeen Shagman

HOW-TO:

Loomwork basics, page 104; making fringe, page 22; attaching fringe, page 63; making a continuous necklace, page 20.

YOU WILL NEED

Beading thread

Bead loom

Seed beads, size 11

Beading needle

Accent beads for fringe and necklace

Bead glue

Muslin

Leather

1 String the loom with 26 warps.

2 The finished piece is 45 rows long. When folded in half lengthwise, both front and back are 22 rows long; one row is taken up by the bottom.

3 Weave the strip according to the pattern, positioning a dragonfly on both front and back of the purse. Feel free to weave a fly of a different color on each side.

4 Before cutting the weaving from the loom, glue a strip of muslin 1/2 inch (1.5 cm) wide across the warps, just above the last beaded row. Allow to dry.

5 Cut beading off the loom just above the muslin strips. Fold the strips to the wrong side of the purse and glue them down.

6 Cut a piece of leather the same size as the beadwork strip. Glue the beadwork to the leather. When dry, trim off any excess leather.

7 Fold the piece in half lengthwise. To make the sides, thread a needle with about 4 feet (1.23 m) of thread. Take the thread through the top row of beads on the front of the pouch. Pick up three seed beads, then needle through the top row on the back. Pick up three more beads and needle through the top row of the front a second time. See Figure 1. Pull thread tight and knot it to the outside warp. Repeat for remaining rows until you reach the bottom. (An alternative to constant knotting: after adding the second set of three beads to the top row, continue around the row again for three or four beads, then needle down to the second row and double back, and so on down the side.)

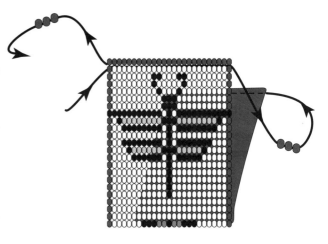

FIGURE 1

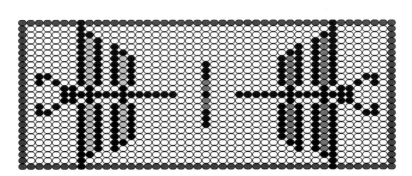

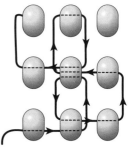

FIGURE 2

8 If you want extra tightness and security, secure each side row to the row above it by zigzagging up the side. See Figure 2.

9 Add the fringe, attaching it to the bottom row.

10 Add the neck strap, finishing it as a continuous loop.

BEADED NECK BAND ON CHAMOIS

This traditional-looking band is tied around the neck, as a choker. It can also serve as a headband, with the ends tied behind the head.

DESIGN:

Nancy McGaha

HOW-TO:

Basic loomwork, page 104; making fringe, page 22.

YOU WILL NEED

Beading thread

Bead loom

Beading needle

Seed beads, size 11

Chamois cloth

Glue

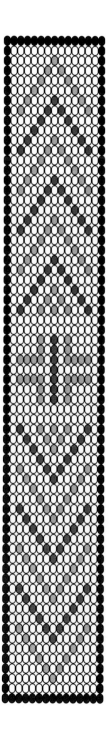

1 String 16 warps on a bead loom.

2 Cut a piece of thread about 1 yard (.9 m) long and tie it to the outer left warp, about 4 inches (10.5 cm) from the bottom of the loom.

3 Working left to right and bottom to top, complete the pattern shown.

4 When the pattern is complete, remove the piece from the loom by cutting the warp threads close to the loom ends, leaving 4-inch strands on the neck band. Tie the warps together by twos or fours. Fold the warps to the back of the neck band, out of the way.

5 Thread the needle with a new piece of thread. Anchor it in the beading and make the fringe. Repeat for other end.

6 Cut a piece of chamois cloth as wide as the beading and a comfortable length for tying around your neck.

7 Glue the beadwork in the center of the chamois cloth.

GEOMETRIC NECKLACE

"MOVING ON," DESIGNER CAROL WILCOX WELLS CALLS THIS PIECE DONE IN FIVE RICH SHADES OF CYLINDER BEADS—BLUE BLACK, BLUE GRAY, MATTE BURGUNDY, SHINY CRANBERRY, AND METALLIC GOLD.

DESIGN:

Carol Wilcox Wells

HOW-TO:

Looming basics, page 104; making fringe, page 22

YOU WILL NEED

Bead loom

Beading thread

Beading needle

Cylinder beads, size 11

1 String the loom with 65 warps. Position the weaving to leave at least 6 inches (15.5 cm) of excess warp threads at the top of the completed piece and 12 inches (31 cm) at the bottom.

2 Note that the bottom of the piece has seven "stairsteps": one in the center and three on each side. Since decreasing the width of the rows is easier than increasing them, the simplest approach is to turn the loom around with the lower end at the top; then, starting in the middle, weave "up" the lower half of the piece. When you've finished, turn the loom back around and weave up the top half of the piece.

If you'd rather weave all the way from bottom to top, begin weaving at the bottom left of the center step and increase the rows as necessary.

3 The stairsteps at the top are less complicated. Weave the last row that runs the full width of the piece. Then weave up the left half of the top, simply stopping the right side of each row where you want it to end. After completing the top left half of the piece, tie on a new thread to the right of the gap in the center, and weave the rows as wide as you want them. Weave up to where the strap narrows.

4 Before you cut the weaving off the loom, run a piece of masking tape across the warps, to keep them separated and untangled. Cut the threads, leaving the excess described in Step 1.

5 At the top, bury the warp threads in the weaving.

6 At the bottom, fringe every other warp and bury the others in the weaving.

7 To avoid a super-long loom, weave the narrow strap separately and stitch it onto the top of the piece.

SPLIT-LOOMED NECKLACE

A TRADITIONAL DESIGN, A SPLIT-LOOMED NECKLACE IS VERY EASY TO MAKE.

DESIGN:

B. J. Crawford

HOW-TO:

Loomwork basics, page 104; making fringe, page 22; using bead tips, page 15.

YOU WILL NEED

Bead loom

Beading thread

Seed beads, size 11

Seed beads, size 8 (for the fringe)

Beading needle

2 bead tips

Spring clasp

1 String the loom with 18 warps, each 30 inches (77 cm) long.

2 Start weaving at the bottom of the necklace. Leave 8 inches (20.5 cm) of bare warp below the first row for the fringe you will make later.

3 Weave 19 rows across all warps. (The rows will be 17 beads wide.)

4 When you reach row 20, weave up the left half of the necklace; the rows of this half are eight beads wide. To create a slanted top, drop one bead on the outside edge in each of the last five rows.

5 Now go back and weave the right side of the necklace—that is, tie on a new thread at warp #10 (counting from left to right) and proceed up the necklace. Again, drop an outside bead on each of the last five rows.

6 Cut the necklace from the loom, leaving the warps as long as possible.

7 To begin the bottom fringe, tie the warps together in square knots as follows: tie warps #1 and #2 together; leave #3 single; knot #4 with #5; leave #6; knot #7 with #8; leave #9; leave #10; knot #11 with #12; leave #13; knot #14 with #15; leave #16; knot #17 with #18.

8 As you string the fringe, treat each pair of knotted warps as one—that is, thread the needle onto both warps, make the dangle, and bury both warps in the weaving. Use size 8 beads next to last in each fringe, for weight.

9 The necklace hangs from 10 strands of beads, five on each side. Tie the top warps together as follows: knot #1 and #2 together; knot #3 with #4; leave #5 single; knot #6 with #7; knot #8 with #9. Make a similar pattern on the other side. Treating the knotted warps as one, string the beads, making them as long as you want. (As shown, the strands are 20 inches, or 51.5 cm, long.)

10 On each side, thread the warps through a bead tip and knot them. Apply a drop of bead glue, allow to dry, and close the tip. Attach a spring clasp.

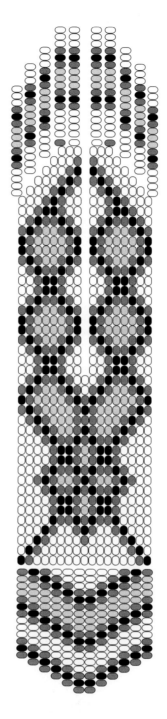

FLAME NECKLACE

INSTEAD OF USING LOOSE STRANDS OF BEADS ONLY AT TOP AND BOTTOM, DESIGN-
ER FRIEDA BATES INTERSPERSES THEM WITH AREAS OF LOOMWORK.

DESIGN:

Frieda Bates

HOW-TO:

*Looming basics, page
104; increasing rows,
page 106; making
fringe, page 22.*

YOU WILL NEED

Bead loom 4 feet
(1.23 m) long

Beading thread

Beading needle

Seed beads, size 14

Ruler

Accent beads for fringe

Bead cement

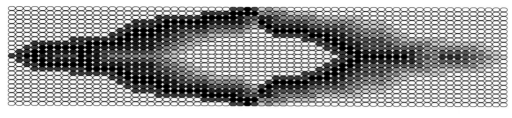

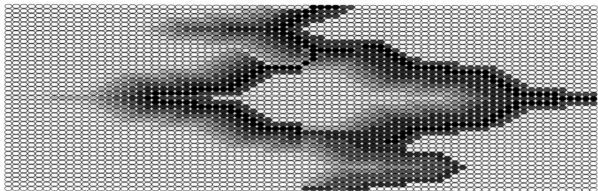

1 Cut 25 pieces of beading thread 12 feet (3.69 m) long. Double each one, to make 50 6-foot (1.8 m) warp threads. Tie the doubled centers to one end of the loom. (When the warps are tied to the loom at both ends, you should end up with a working area about 4 feet long.)

2 String about 17 inches (43.5 cm) of beads onto each warp. Push them down to the far end of the loom. Tie the other ends of the warp to the loom, making sure you can untie them later.

3 First loom the bottom pendant. Start at the bottom row and loom your way up. Alternatively, if you don't want to increase that many rows, start at the widest part of the pendant and weave to the bottom of the pendant; then turn the loom around weave up the remaining rows to the top.

4 After you have woven the pendant, slide the desired number of beads down from the other end of the loom, pushing them snugly against the pendant. The more you add, the longer the necklace. Make sure the tops of the strung beads are absolutely even. (Don't count the beads, since they vary in size; lay the ruler across the warps to make sure the line is straight.)

5 Separate the warps into two groups and begin weaving the strap on the left side of the necklace, working from bottom to top. As you finish weaving each row, slide down more beads on each side of the weaving to cover the warps. When you finish the left strap, weave the right one.

6 Slide the next group of beads down against the weaving.

7 Weave the final portion of the strap—the rectangle that appears at the back of the neck.

8 Remove the piece from the loom by cutting the looped warps at the top end and untying the warps at the pendant end. Discard any extra beads from the top of the warps.

9 Join the back of the necklace by tying each pair of warp thread together—a warp from one side with a warp from the other side. Dot the knots with bead glue or clear nail polish. For each pair of warps, clip one thread right above the knot and string fringe on the other, burying the warp ends in the weaving.

10 Below the pendant, string beads on the warps to make fringe, burying the ends in the weaving.

LOOMED NECKLACE WITH COMANCHE TRIM

DESIGNER GINI WILLIAMS ADDED AN UNUSUAL TWIST TO THIS STUDY IN BRONZE, CREAM, AND RED. SHE FINISHED THE OUTSIDE EDGES WITH A ROW OF COMANCHE WEAVE.

DESIGN:

Gini Williams

HOW-TO:

Looming basics, page 104; increasing rows, page 106; making fringe, page 22; Comanche weave, page 98.

YOU WILL NEED

Bead loom

Bead thread

Hex-cut seed beads, size 15

Beading needle

Bugle beads and accent beads (for fringe)

1 String 52 warps that are about 6 feet (1.8 m) long, giving you a working area of about 4 feet (1.23 m).

2 When positioning your weaving on the warps, leave at least 16 inches (41 cm) of bare warp at the bottom for the fringe you will string later; leave at least 12 inches (31 cm) bare at the top, for the strands.

3 Begin by looming the central medallion. Since decreasing the width of the rows is easier than increasing them, work from the top of the medallion to the bottom.

4 Now turn the loom around and weave the left-hand strap, this time working from bottom to top. When that's finished, tie on a new weft and weave the right-hand strap. Make the straps as long as you like.

5 Remove the beadwork from the loom. At the top, string seed beads onto each warp and attach the findings. At the bottom, make fringe and work the ends back into the woven medallion.

6 Now make the short fringe around the piece. If you look closely at an outside edge of loomed bead-work, you will see the outermost warp connecting the rows of beads. If you turn the work sideways, with the warps running horizontally, you'll see a perfect base for Comanche weave.

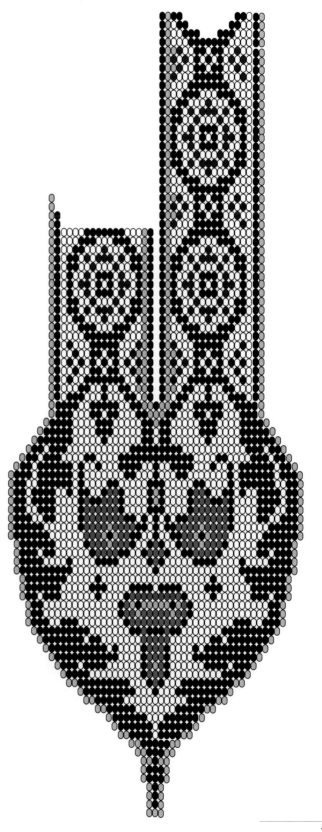

A S C A R A B
C L A S P I S A
F I N E F I N I S H

7 To make the Comanche weave, string on a seed bead. Take the needle under a loop of warp thread, then back through the seed bead. Now string on a bugle bead and another seed bead. Needle back through the bugle, add another seed bead, and go through the next loop of warp thread. See Figure 1. Continue in this way until you've encircled the entire piece.

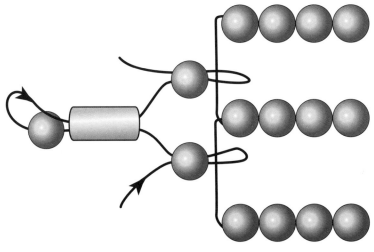

FIGURE 1

"Full Chat"

DESIGN:

Jeanette Ahlgren

TEE NECKLACES

These stunning loomed necklaces, shaped like the letter T, are by Jeanette Ahlgren. They are woven in two sections, stitched together, and backed with leather.

"Deco" displays a technique for which Ahlgren is well known: a gradual transition from one color to another, in this case from dark brown to gold to wheat. Her technique, which she calls "random dot bleed," involves gradually adding more of the new color and less of the old to each row, working in a random pattern. Ahlgren doesn't plan or graph the color shifts; rather, she picks up beads of a different color as the spirit moves her.

"Deco"

DESIGN:

Jeanette Ahlgren

MAKING BEADS

Once, of course, all beads were handmade. Even now, with gorgeous mass-produced beads everywhere available, it's still fun to make your own. Paper, fabric, wood, bamboo—all make delightful beads.

POLYMER CLAY

Perhaps the most popular homemade beads are polymer clay, a relatively new modeling compound that's inexpensive, easy to use, and incredibly versatile.

Available in most craft stores, polymer clay comes in 2-ounce (60 g) blocks in a riot of colors. Small pieces can be rolled into balls and baked in a home oven to produce hard, durable beads.

Begin by kneading the clay in your hands, to soften it and make it pliable. Then shape it however you want. Use your hands to make round, square, oval, or wafer beads, exactly as you shaped modeling clay in kindergarten. Roll out a long "snake," or log, then slice it with a razor craft knife to make

After shaping the beads, pierce each one with a needle or straight pin to make a hole. Thread the beads onto wooden or metal skewers and rest the skewers across a baking pan. Bake the beads at the time and temperature recommended by the manufacturer—usually between 265° F and 275° F (130° C to 135° C) for 10 to 30 minutes. Check the label on each package, since colors can vary.

If the available colors aren't exactly what you want, you can create your own. If you knead two colors together long enough, they will blend into a third.

Making a Snail

Roll a log of clay about 2 inches (5 cm) long—thick in the center and tapering gradually to the ends. Coil up both ends until they meet in the middle, then press the two center coils gently together. Pierce the bead between the center coils.

Making a Jellyroll

Named for the famous cake, this playful pattern is easy to make. Knead two (or more) colors of clay to soften them. With a rolling pin or brayer, roll them into thin, flat sheets. Lay one sheet on top of the other and roll them gently to seal them. Trim away excess clay to make a rectangle about 3 by 4 inches (7.5 x 10.5 cm). Starting with a short end, roll the sheets up into a log. See Figure 1. Slice off the uneven ends of the log and discard them. Slice the remainder of the log into even slices. Pierce the beads from edge to edge and bake them.

COLORFUL
BLOCKS OF
POLYMER CLAY

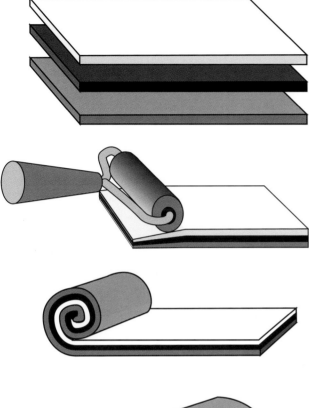

slices and use your hand to compress them together into one loaf. See Figure 2. Slice the loaf into beads of equal thickness. Pierce the beads from edge to edge (or from corner to corner) and bake them according to the package instructions.

SAFETY

To be on the safe side, it's a good idea to avoid using the same implements (e.g., rolling pins) for polymer clay and for food. Make sure to have adequate ventilation when the beads are baking.

READ ON

An excellent introduction to polymer clay jewelry is Leslie Dierks' *Creative Clay Jewelry* (Asheville, NC: Lark Books, 1994).

FIGURE 1

Making a Checkerboard

Checkerboard beads complement a variety of jewelry styles. To make them, use the rolling pin to make four flat sheets of clay. Stack the sheets on top of each other, alternating colors. Trim the edges to make a rectangular loaf, then cut the loaf into four equal slices. Alternate the direction of the four

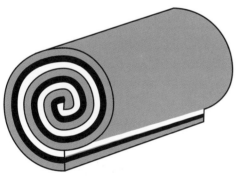

FIGURE 2

BROWN BAG NECKLACE

THE PRIMITIVE GEOMETRIC DESIGNS ON THESE PAPER BEADS WERE APPLIED WITH A
FELT-TIPPED MARKER.

DESIGN:

Ellen Zahorec

HOW-TO:

Clasps, page 15.

YOU WILL NEED

Brown paper
grocery bag

Scissors

Knitting needle

Glue

Black felt-tipped
marker

Wooden spacer beads

Waxed cord or leather
thong

Brass coils

Chain-nose pliers

Clasp

1 Cut strips of brown paper bag 1 inch (2.5 cm) wide and 4 to 8 inches (10.5-20.5 cm) long, depending on how fat you want the bead.

2 Fold over 1/4 inch (1 cm) of paper to the wrong side on each long edge; you should have a strip 1/2 inch (1.5 cm) wide.

3 Roll the strip around the knitting needle, as tightly as possible and glue the end to the bead. (To make

a narrower bead, just cut narrower strips of paper.)

4 Using the felt-tipped marker, blacken the ends of the beads and decorate them with lines, dots, and squiggles.

5 String the beads on the cord or leather. Add a coil at each end. With the pliers, mash a few coils next to the beads, to hold the coil on the cord. Attach the parts of the clasp to the coils.

MARBLED PAPER NECKLACE

DESIGNER LAURA SIMS IS A PROFESSIONAL MARBLER WHO'S ALWAYS LOOKING FOR THINGS TO DO WITH HER HANDSOME PAPERS. BEADS ARE A GOOD SOLUTION.

1 Cut elongated triangles of paper—4 to 7 inches (10.5-18 cm) long, about 1 inch (2.5 cm) wide at the base and narrowing to a point.

2 With right side out and starting at the wide end, roll the pieces of paper around the needle. Glue the end to the bead and set aside to dry.

3 Lay the beads and chips out in the desired order. String the beads and chips and attach the clasp.

DESIGN:

Laura Sims

HOW-TO:

Clasps, page 15.

YOU WILL NEED

Marbled or other decorative paper

Scissors

Knitting needle or large head pin

Glue

Mineral chips

Beading thread

Beading needle

Clasp

FAUX JADE NECKLACE

VERSATILE POLYMER CLAY CAN MIMIC A VARIETY OF MINERALS AND SEMIPRECIOUS STONES. HERE IT SPANS THE COLOR RANGE OF JADE.

DESIGN:

Susan Kinney

HOW-TO:

Polymer clay basics, page 128.

YOU WILL NEED

1 block translucent polymer clay

1/16 block green

1/16 block tan

1/16 block purple or dark blue

1/8 block black

Brown potting soil

Black leather cord

Fine grit sandpaper

1 Knead the clay until it is pliable and easily shaped.

2 Pull off half a block of translucent clay. Mix into it a small piece of green about 1/4 inch (1 cm) wide. Check the mixture's color; if it needs more green, add another piece. Roll the mixture into balls about 1 inch (2.5 cm) in diameter.

3 Divide the remaining translucent clay into three pieces. Set one piece aside. Into the second piece mix two or three small tan balls 1/8 inch (.5 cm) across. Into the third piece, mix a tiny ball (1/8 inch or so) of dark blue or purple.

4 Using tiny amounts of green, tan, and blue clay, press into very thin sheets of various sizes and apply them to the balls, pressing them gently into place. The object is to vary the colors in the "jade," mimicking nature's imperfections.

5 To simulate the flecks of mica that appear in jade, crumble tiny specks of black clay and roll a few into each ball. Sprinkle a little potting soil onto your work table and roll the beads in it. If the dark specks loom too large and obvious, cover them with thin pieces of translucent clay.

6 Roll the balls well on a smooth surface, to remove finger marks.

7 Form the balls into beads of various shapes: a square doughnut, some wafer beads, and some long cylinder beads. If necessary, vary the colors by adding more thin sheets of the tan or purple mixture.

8 Pierce each bead with a needle to make a hole. Preheat the oven to 20˚ F (11˚ C) higher than the manufacturer's recommended baking temperature. Put the beads in the oven, then immediately turn the oven down to the recommended temperature. Do not overbake; translucent clay browns if baked too long.

9 When the beads are done, let them cool in the oven. If bumps have appeared in the beads, sand them lightly with 600 grit sandpaper. (Wear a mask when sanding.)

10 String the beads on the leather cord, knotting on each side of the beads to hold them in place.

MARBLED BARREL BEADS

COMBINE ANY COLORS YOU LIKE TO PRODUCE A RAINBOW-HUED NECKLACE
AND EARRINGS.

DESIGN:

Tamela Wells Laity

HOW-TO:

*Polymer basics,
page 128; crimp beads,
page 15; head
pins, page 13.*

YOU WILL NEED

Polymer clay in various
colors

Craft knife

Tigertail

Silver spacer beads

Heart-shaped bead
(optional)

2 crimp beads

Clasp

2 head pins

Silver ear wires

1 Collect clay in various colors. Cut it up into pieces
about 1/8 inch (3 mm) in diameter. Gather the
pieces up in a ball and squeeze them together until
most of the air pockets have been removed. Be careful not to knead the clay too long, or the colors will
obediently blend together into one uniform hue.

2 Roll the clay into a log about 1/2 inch (1.5 cm)
in diameter.

3 Twist the log from each end in opposite directions, then roll it in your hands to smooth it. Twist
again until the lines are interesting. Roll the log on
your work surface until it is as small as you want it.

4 Cut the log into barrel-shaped beads of equal length.

5 Stick a straight pin lengthwise through each bead
to make a hole.

6 Bake the beads according the package instructions. Allow to cool.

7 To make the necklace, string the polymer beads
on the tigertail, alternating with silver spacers. Add
a heart-shaped accent bead, if desired, and a
clasp.

8 To make the earrings, string a silver spacer, then
a barrel bead, then another spacer onto a head pin
and attach the head pin to the ear wire. Repeat for
other earring.

SHOW-OFF POLYMER NECKLACE

ONCE YOU'VE MADE TWO DIFFERENT KINDS OF POLYMER BEADS, WHY NOT WEAR THEM BOTH? THIS EXUBERANT SET COMBINES JELLYROLL AND CHECKERBOARD BEADS TO GOOD EFFECT.

1 Make jellyroll beads with the pink and purple clay. Make checkerboard beads with the black and white.

2 Bake all beads according to package instructions and allow to cool.

3 To assemble the necklace, string the polymer beads and the accent beads on the tigertail, follow-ing the pattern in the photo or creating your own. Finish with the crimp beads and the clasp.

4 To make the earrings, string the beads on the head pins as shown and attach the head pins to the ear wires.

DESIGN:

Tamela Wells Laity

HOW-TO:

Polymer basics, page 128; making jellyroll beads, page 128; making checkerboard beads, page 129; crimp beads, page 15.

YOU WILL NEED

Polymer clay in pink, purple, black, and white

Silver bugle beads

Silver spacers and wafer beads

Blue glass spacers

Teal spacers

Tigertail

Heart-shaped accent bead (optional)

Crimp beads

Clasp

2 head pins

2 ear wires

BLACK AND WHITE EARRINGS

OF ALL THE COLORS AVAILABLE IN POLYMER CLAY, BLACK AND WHITE ARE TWO OF THE MOST EFFECTIVE. THIS PATTERN IS SIMPLY A JELLYROLL THAT IS CUT LENGTHWISE AND REASSEMBLED.

DESIGN:

Irene Dean

HOW-TO:

Polymer basics, page 128; making a jellyroll, page 128; head pins, page 13.

YOU WILL NEED

Black clay

White clay

Rolling pin

Sharp knife

Accent beads

2 head pins

2 ear wires

Round-nose pliers

1 Tear off a piece of white clay and a piece of black, and knead each one to make it pliable. Roll a thin sheet of black and a thin sheet of white. Place the black sheet on top of the white and trim away the edges, to make a rectangle about 3 by 4 inches (7.5 x 10.5 cm). Starting with a short side, roll the sheets up into a jellyroll.

2 Roll the jellyroll log on your work surface until it's about 6 inches (15.5 cm) long. Cut off a 2-inch (5 cm) section and set aside. Roll the remaining log until it's half as wide as it was; cut off two more 2-inch sections. Roll the log until it's reduced by half again; cut off six additional 2-inch sections.

3 Carefully cut each section in half lengthwise. You will have a total of 18 halves with half-spiral patterns.

4 Lay one of the large halves on your work surface, cut side down. Place a little white clay on top of it, then place the other large half log on top of the first, also cut side down. See Figure 1.

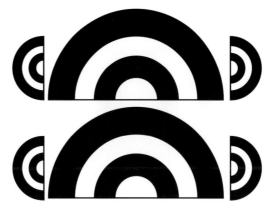

FIGURE 2

5 Place the four medium-sized halves on each side of the large ones. See Figure 2.

6 Roll a thin sheet of white clay and surround your creation so far. Position the remaining small halves around the perimeter, placing six on each side. Fill in the holes with long, thin rolls of white clay, to make a semicircular loaf.

7 Gently compress the entire log with your hands, to firm up the components and smooth the outside.

8 Roll out two sheets of black clay and one of white. Wrap your log with a sheet of black, then of white, then black again.

9 Let the cane rest until it's firm again. Then cut it into slices about 1/4 inch (7 mm) thick. Pierce each bead top to bottom and bake according to manufacturer's instructions.

10 To assemble the earrings, string a silver spacer onto a head pin, then a polymer bead, then a matte glass bead and another silver spacer. Attach the head pin to an ear wire.

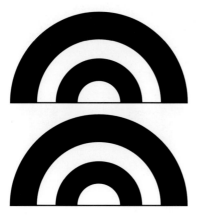

FIGURE 1

DENIM BEADS

Don these playful beads with jeans and shirt, and you've got a conversation opener for your next picnic or barbecue. Fabric paints and glazes are available at craft stores and discount marts.

DESIGN:

Barbara Evans

HOW-TO:

Adding a clasp,
page 15.

YOU WILL NEED

Used denim jeans

Hollow plastic coffee stirrers

Fabric glue

Wooden toothpicks

Plastic foam strip

Dimensional squeeze-bottle fabric paint

Clear fabric glaze

Soft brush

Spacer beads

Beading thread

Beading needle

Clasp

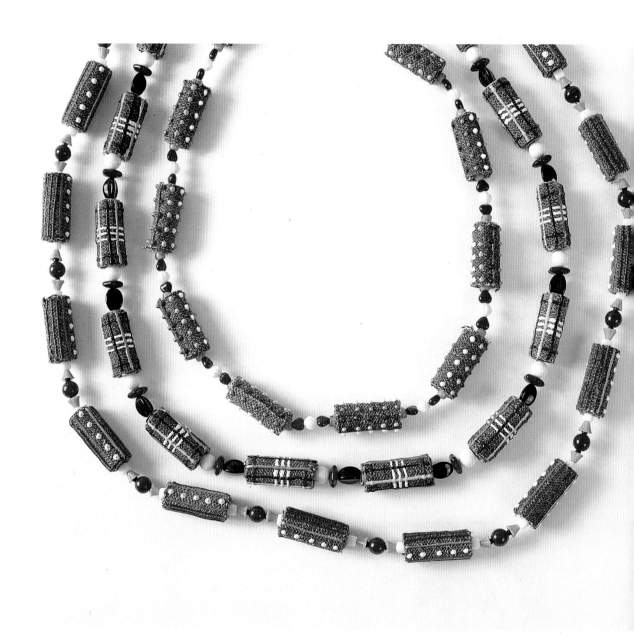

1 Because new denim yardage frays easily, it doesn't work well for these beads. Use old jeans instead.

2 For each bead, cut a piece of denim 1-1/2 inches by 4 or 5 inches (4 by 10.5 or 13 cm). For smaller beads, cut narrower pieces.

3 Cut a piece of coffee stirrer about 2 inches (5 cm) long.

4 Place a fabric piece wrong side up and apply glue as shown in Figure 1.

5 Lay stirrer on glued section and roll fabric around stirrer as tightly as possible. See Figure 2. Press end together for a few seconds. Repeat with remaining fabric pieces.

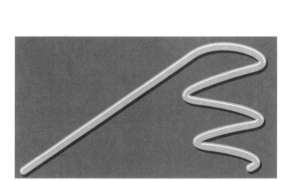

FIGURE 1

6 Insert a cocktail pick in each bead and stick the pick in the foam.

7 Holding a bead by the pick, decorate it with squeeze bottle paint, using whatever colors and patterns occur to you. Stick the bead back into the foam to dry. If you're using more than one layer of paint, allow each layer to dry before applying another.

8 After paint is completely dry, dip each bead in fabric glaze. Wipe off excess with a soft brush and allow to dry.

9 Lay out the beads and the spacers in the desired order. String the beads and attach the clasp.

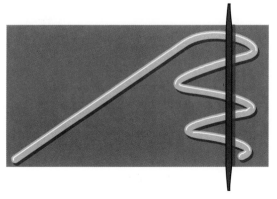

FIGURE 2

BAMBOO CHOKER

TRADITIONAL NATIVE AMERICAN CHOKERS ARE MADE WITH BONE HAIRPIPES. THIS ONE IS MADE WITH BAMBOO HARVESTED ALONG A NEIGHBOR'S CREEK. A RICH GREEN WHEN HARVESTED, THE BAMBOO WILL WEATHER INTO A PALE, HANDSOME BROWN.

DESIGN:

Barry Olen

HOW-TO:

*Making a wire loop,
page 45.*

YOU WILL NEED

Bamboo

Leather scraps

Heavy scissors or
razor knife

Awl

2 pieces of flat leather
thong 1 foot (31 cm)
long

African turquoise disks

Red whiteheart beads

Beading thread

Beading needle

22-gauge silver wire

Wire cutters

Bone doughnut

Feather

Leather glue or
craft glue

1 Harvest thin, pliable pieces of bamboo of equal diameter. Cut them into 2-inch (5 cm) lengths, making sure that there are no bamboo joints on any of your beads. Each joint marks an interior membrane that would prevent the bead from being strung.

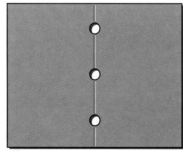

FIGURE 1

2 To make the leather spacers that will separate the necklace into five segments, cut out four leather ovals slightly longer than the intended width of the choker. With the awl, punch three equidistant holes down the length of the spacer. See Figure 1.

3 Cut two leather rectangles about 2 inches by 3 inches (5 x 7.5 cm) for the tabs at each end.

4 String three strands of beads, following the pattern shown in the photo.

5 Fold a leather tab in half lengthwise and pencil a mark along the fold on the wrong side of the leather. With the awl, punch three holes along the line. See Figure 2.

FIGURE 2

6 Thread a needle onto one end of a strand of beads. Moving from right side to wrong side, take the needle through one of the holes on the tab. Knot the thread on the wrong side of the tab. Attach the other two strands of beads in a similar manner. Repeat for the other tab.

7 Fold each leather tab in half, wrong sides together, and trim off the corners as desired. Place a line of glue around the edge of the wrong side of each leather tab and glue the sides together. Allow to dry.

8 Now make the strap. Near the end of each tab, make a slit through both thicknesses of leather, wide enough to admit the leather thong. See Figure 3. Cut one end of each thong at an angle to make a

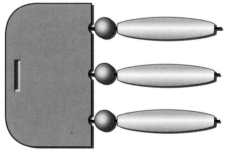

FIGURE 3

point, and cut a slit in the other end. See Figure 4. Insert the pointed end of the thong through the slit in the tab and pull the thong most of the way through. Take the pointed end through the slit in the thong's other end and pull it snug. See Figure 5.

9 To attach the doughnut, first carve a groove around the center piece of bamboo. Wrap a piece of wire around that groove, add the doughnut and a turquoise disk, and form the wire into a loop.

10 Cut a second piece of wire and make a loop in one end. String on the feather and three beads. Make a loop in the other end, attaching it to the loop in the center of the doughnut.

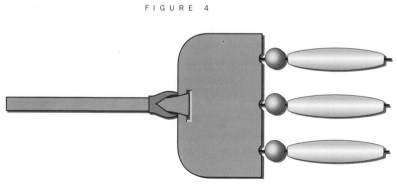

FIGURE 4

FIGURE 5

CONTRIBUTING DESIGNERS

Kimberley Adams is a glass bead maker and jewelry designer who combines her lamp-worked beads with wire fashioned of precious metals. Her work is shown in various galleries and shops.

Jeanette Ahlgren is a former painter who now works in beads. Her current beadwork consists of "Structures"—freestanding, three-dimensional forms. Her work has appeared in numerous galleries, collections, and publications.

Melanie Alter is a founder of the New Mexico Bead Society and a jewelry designer who utilizes beads, charms, and findings from around the world. In addition to her one-of-a-kind creations, she markets beads and ornamentation through a mail-order catalog (505/298-7036).

Frieda Bates specializes in loomed jewelry. Many of her pieces reflect the New Mexican landscape where she resides. Her work has appeared in various publications and galleries.

Leslie Bruntsch teaches beadwork at The Shepherdess in San Diego, California, and in the San Diego public schools.

B. J. Crawford is co-owner of Earth Guild, a craft store and mail-order supplier in Asheville, North Carolina (704/255-7818). Although she enjoys beadwork, she is primarily a weaver and basketmaker.

Irene Dean is a polymer clay artist and teacher. She markets her work directly from her studio—good night irene!—in Asheville, North Carolina, and at craft shows and shops.

Erin Everett strings and wires beads to produce one-of-a-kind jewelry, which she markets at craft fairs.

Barbara Evans is primarily a cloth dollmaker, but she also loves beads, especially African trade beads. To combine her two interests, she makes beads from fabric.

Patti Hill, formerly a New Orleans restauranteur, is now an organic farmer, basketmaker, beader, weaver, and all-around crafter.

Susan Kinney is a papermaker, potter, jeweler, and interior designer.

Tamela Wells Laity began her professional life as a silversmith. Then she discovered polymer clay—before any authors or teachers did—and developed her own designs and techniques for the new material. She is a full-time studio artist in polymer clay.

Lonnie Lovness finds her inspiration in extensive travel; she is fascinated by exotic places and components. Her jewelry is marketed in shops across the country.

Galen Madaras taught herself jewelry making while she was living in the mountains of Arkansas. Her admiration for the art of native peoples around the world influences her designs and materials.

Collis Marshall was a painter and professional seamstress before she discovered beads, and her earlier avocations have influenced the patterns and colors in her beadwork. She travels extensively, collecting textiles from around the world and studying ancient bead-weaving techniques.

Nancy McGaha has been making loomed bead jewelry for about two years. Formerly enthralled by all kinds of needlecraft—crochet and smocking, especially—she is now addicted to beadwork. Her colorful bracelets are sold in craft shops and galleries.

Madison MacLaren is a potter by profession and a beader by inclination. Her ceramic works are sold and collected nationwide; her necklaces of strung beads are presents to herself and her friends.

NanC Meinhardt came to beadwork through bookbinding. For years she used beads to embellish books. As time went on, she became more interested in the beads than in the books.

Lynn Nelson has always been fascinated by beads. (She is confident that, if she had previous lives, she was the tribal beader then as well.) She delights in teaching people to make jewelry, watching their dawning realization that they can create something beautiful.

Jana Hunt Newton is a jewelry designer whose work ranges from ethnic to Victorian. Her work appears in various collections and galleries.

Barry Olen is fascinated by the history and manufacture of beads. He is the owner of Beads and Beyond, a bead store in Asheville, North Carolina.

Pat Poole-Frank is known primarily for her off-loom weaving, but she also makes a popular line of strung and wired jewelry.

Margaret Reed indulges in a variety of crafts, including beadwork. She not only strings beads but makes peyote pouches as well.

Cynthia Rutledge is a jewelry designer and teacher of beading. Her work is shown in a variety of galleries and shops.

Janeen Shagman says the measured, methodical pace of off-loom weaving suits her nature: her beading is a time of tranquility and introspection. She also enjoys pottery, sculpting, and stained glass.

Kimberly Shuck took her degree in Art Textiles but has since branched out into numerous other fields. In addition to beadwork, she enjoys basketry, feltmaking, weaving, and tatting. She is also a published poet.

Laura Sims is a professional marbler and teacher of marbling. Her studio, Indigo Stone, is in Asheville, North Carolina. She was a creative consultant for the book *Marbling Paper and Fabric* (Sterling Publishing, 1991).

Mary Young Smith is a weaver, basketmaker, and beader who has taught all three crafts to more students than she can remember.

Jody Stewart-Keller became interested in beadweaving because of her Ojibwa heritage, but she's now enthralled with beading for its own sake. She works primarily in peyote stitch.

Marcie Stone's beadwork has appeared in numerous galleries, collections, and publications. She is perhaps best known for her combinations of beadwork and pine-needle basketry. She is the owner of The Shepherdess, a fine bead shop in San Diego, California, which offers a series of classes taught by talented beaders.

Cheri Lynn Waltz is a jewelry designer who teaches beadwork of various kinds. She is a frequent contributor to *Bead and Button* magazine.

Virginia Wayne works with beads in a variety of ways. She is particularly fond of silver and brass wire and constantly finds new ways to combine them with beads. She also makes and markets peyote pouches.

Carol Wilcox Wells has been in the graphic arts for two decades. Originally a painter, she began adding beads to her painted canvases. When there were more beads than paint, she decided to switch media. Now a full-time beader and teacher of beading, she also runs a mail-order business, stocking (among other things) delica beads in a fine assortment of colors (704/252-0274).

Gini Williams is an award-winning beader and jewelry designer whose work appears in a variety of shops and galleries in the U.S. and Japan. She has taught numerous workshops at art and craft centers such as the Penland School in Penland, North Carolina.

Barbara Wright strings beads almost as often as she breathes. She has taught hundreds of people the ins and outs of basic jewelry making.

Sarah K. Young is assistant editor of *Bead and Button* magazine. She also manages the largest bead store in Boston and teaches beading through the Cambridge Continuing Education program.

Ellen Zahorec is a mixed-media studio artist who specializes in handmade paper and collage. Her work has been shown internationally and is part of numerous private and corporate collections.

Donna Zalusky is a glass bead maker and jewelry designer. She is an active member of the Washington Bead Society.

ACKNOWLEDGEMENTS

Thanks to the dozens of people who were indispensable in the preparation of this book.

TEACHING: Mary Young Smith, Jody Stewart-Keller, Virginia Wayne, Barbara Wright, and Carol Wilcox Wells

NETWORKING: Alice Korach, editor of *Bead and Button* magazine; Gabrielle Liese, director of the Bead Museum, Prescott, Arizona; Marcie Stone, owner of Shepherdess, San Diego, California; Mary Fletcher of Farrin and Fletcher Design Studios, Pasadena, California: and Carol Wilcox Wells.

PHOTO PROPS: Barry Olen, owner of Beads and Beyond in Asheville, North Carolina, lent beads, tools, and findings, as well as advice and encouragement. Carol Wilcox Wells lent trays of seed beads from her impressive stock (page 71) and her favorite bead loom, built by Bob Wells (page 109). Rosemary Kast lent her handsome head of hair for the photo on page 59.

ADDITIONAL PHOTOGRAPHY: Pages 82, 90, and 119: Tim Barnwell; Page 127: Alice Scherer

PHOTO STYLING: Photos on pages 32, 47, 49, 51, 59, 60, 61, 110, and 116 were styled by Dana Irwin.

INDEX